AFTERMATH

AFTERMATH

Life in the Shadows of Headlines and History

AAKASH KARKARE

RUPA

First published by
Rupa Publications India Pvt. Ltd 2025
161-B/4, Gulmohar House,
Yusuf Sarai Community Centre,
New Delhi 110049

Sales centres:
Bengaluru Chennai
Hyderabad Kolkata Mumbai

The views and opinions expressed in this book are the author's own and the facts are as reported by him; these have been verified to the extent possible, and the publishers are not in any way liable for the same.

P-ISBN: 978-93-7003-787-8
E-ISBN: 978-93-7003-917-9

First impression 2025

10 9 8 7 6 5 4 3 2 1

Printed in India

Artie, who I rescued from the rain, and who, in turn, rescued me from the storm within

Contents

Part I

A Night Without End
(2008–09)

'The past, like a severed limb,
tried to fix itself onto the body of the present.'

—Hisham Matar, *The Return*

1

The boy whose dad got shot

At thirty-four, I've spent almost half my life trying not to be defined by a single night in 2008. It has proved to be quite difficult, since that event has had an interminably long public afterlife. It is often the first thing people think about when they hear my last name. An annoying spark of recognition flashes across their faces when the connection has been made, and I am dragged into a conversation I have been trying to avoid for almost two decades now.

These reminders of my past arrive at the most innocuous moments: during an early morning walk in the neighbourhood park; while accepting a delivery of groceries; while getting my internet connection installed; while having my blood drawn; while interacting with strangers on chess.com or on dating apps. And they arrive at the most inconvenient times too: from a colleague in the urinal next to me at work, or at the front of a government office queue for an Aadhaar card, or during a passport renewal after sweating in the Mumbai sun for two hours.

On each occasion, I am turned into a spectacle for the onlookers: '*Come look, he's Karkare's son. The boy whose dad got shot.*'

My defence mechanism against these intrusions is to hide my surname as much as possible and avoid conversations involving my parents or my family life. But this very circumspection creates its own kind of mystery.

'*Why didn't you tell us before?*' people ask when they find out. I am always unsure how to respond. Am I supposed to walk into rooms and announce to all and sundry: 'My name is Aakash. My dad died in a terrorist attack several years ago. I prefer not to talk about it?'

In my twenties, encounters of this nature would send me into paroxysms of rage. It happens less now, but each time, I find myself wishing that the process of changing a surname didn't have to involve courts and public notices in newspapers. Or that I could live somewhere without having to remember my past at all.

I'm unsure why mentions of what happened has become such an anathema to me. I've never found comfort in the vocabulary of 'grief' and 'trauma' that seems so common in online discussions on mental health. I am not the kind of person who believes that a life can be reduced to single moments that can haunt you for the rest of your life. That sort of thing belongs to movie tropes, not real life. Or so one would like to believe. And yet, despite all my efforts to outrun the past and sever my ties to it, I have felt its echoes shaping my life, in ways both obvious and obscure.

∽

I was seventeen. It was 26 November 2008. I refuse to call it 26/11, because overuse has drained the phrase of all its meaning. I was sitting on the sofa in the living room of our ground-floor apartment in European Quarters. My sister S, who was living in Leipzig, was on the Skype window open on the laptop in front of me. Our eldest sister, J, who was living in Boston, had logged off a few moments earlier—I can no longer remember why. Mummy was in my parents' bedroom, talking to her mother, Bombay Aaji (to distinguish her from Nagpur Aaji on my father's side), or perhaps to her younger brother, Kiran Mama, on the landline telephone. Bruno, the six-month-old Doberman puppy Pappa had brought home one night, lay with his head in my lap. I'd placed it there when I began watching the news. His warm breath against my skin was calming.

Suddenly, a burst of computer-generated lightning flashed across the television screen. Audio fragments like 'Cama

Hospital', 'Toyota Qualis', 'Kasab' spilled from the TV speakers, passing through my mind without leaving a trace. My eyes fixed instead on the ticker scrolling across the bottom: 'Anti-Terrorist Squad Chief Hemant Karkare has been shot.'

Strangely enough, the first thing I thought of was the fried snack *dal moth*.

I was six when I had carefully packed a giant packet of Lay's Magic Masala chips and a packet of one of my favourite snacks. That night, just before bed, Mummy had called me into the kitchen, where Pappa stood sheepishly with a glass of whisky in hand.

He was a social drinker, seldom prone to indulgence, but there were a few friends in whose company his mask always dropped. One such friend had dropped in unexpectedly, and Pappa wanted to know if he could open the packet of dal moth to have it with his drink. I refused, worried that a half-open packet would make the snack go soggy before I could share it with my friends on the bus the next day. My mother had laughed and teased him, saying, 'I told you he wouldn't let you.'

On the bus ride home, my eyes fell on the dal moth packet, still unopened. I had forgotten all about it amidst all the amusement park rides. Someday, when Pappa died, I remembered thinking to myself, I was going to feel guilty for that unshared packet of *namkeen*. And here I was in the living room of our government-allocated apartment in Dadar TT, thinking about dal moth while hearing myself say to S, 'They are saying Pappa is dead.'

This moment seems perpetually frozen outside of time, and I always observe it from a distance, as if I am not truly a part of it. Because it unfolded on a TV screen, I was unable to believe it. Not that night, nor for several days after. And for a moment that would reverberate through the next decade of my life, I found myself unable to feel anything at all.

This clarity of memory, even after so many years, seems

common in experiences like these, or so the books I've read on similar events would suggest.

Almost seventeen years later, it is not the chaos of that night or the weeks that followed that comes to me first. My mind prefers instead to conjure up the exact shade of light brown of the sofa upholstery I was sitting on. I see the grey Onida television at the centre of the plywood showcase in our living room. I recall the dull whitish-orange glow, a mix of the tube light and the recessed lamps in the drop ceiling above. Through the window near the entrance, I can see the branches of the mahogany tree in our compound, silhouetted against the night sky, barely moving. It felt quite late, though I am unsure of the time. (It was around midnight according to court records I once looked at to jog my memory.[1] That there are court records about an event I consider this personal never ceases to unnerve me.)

It was a Wednesday, something I know without ever having to check a calendar. Long before I found myself sitting on that light-brown couch in front of the TV screen, I went for an early morning German class, one of the many coaching classes I was attending to prepare for my 12th standard board exams the following year. The post-class tradition with my friends was to bunk the day's lectures and catch a discounted matinee at Matunga's Star City Cinema. That day, we saw the action film *Death Race*, starring British actor Jason Statham, and then gorged on the famed *misal pav* at Aaswad for lunch. Pappa came home later that day while I was in the midst of watching India race to a 5–0 lead in the One Day International series against England at the Barabati Stadium in Cuttack.

I've always retained a nostalgic fondness for the first half of this day. Sometimes, I want to reach into it and remember how that before-time felt like. It seems so ordinary, so boring. A last remnant of an innocence I seem to have forever lost. Losing

[1]Md. Ajmal Md. Amir Kasab and Abu Majahid vs. State of Maharashtra, Criminal Appeal Nos. 1899-1900 of 2012, decided on 29 August 2012, Supreme Court of India.

that innocence wasn't a gradual process; it happened in an instant. One day, everything was one way, and the very next day, everything seemed to have changed completely. It makes the regret feel all that more acute.

Pappa changed out of his office wear: black trousers and a light-blue shirt, and into his home attire: light-blue drawstring pajamas and a white sleeveless banyan. He was about to sit down to dinner when his Blackberry buzzed. He went inside to answer it out of earshot, a normal-enough occurrence. Then he emerged from the bedroom, changed back into his office wear, and walked out of the front door without saying where he was going. Communication was never our family's strongest suit. The last sound I remember hearing was the slamming of the doors on his white Tata Indigo and the wrought-iron gates of our compound being dragged open to let him leave.

I'm not sure why the mind holds on to everyday details, particularly on days that do not seem like they belong to the everyday. Perhaps there's something comforting about the mundane in chaotic times, a reminder that even in the face of massive upheaval, most of our lives are made of small, everyday gestures of living.

That is at least how I like to think of my life: mostly normal, not marked by what others might call tragedy. Not absurd, not particularly unlucky. That I don't need to perform archaic rituals to chase away evil energies, as a university professor once advised after Mummy died six years later.

When I returned to the sofa, I discovered that the cricket series had been cancelled midway, prompting me to switch from Ten Sports to Times Now. Shootings had been reported at Chhatrapati Shivaji Terminus (CST), the Taj, the Oberoi, the Trident, and around Metro Cinema. Bombs had gone off in taxis in Vile Parle and Mazgaon. At first, reports suggested gang fighting, until it was revealed that a group of terrorists had descended on Mumbai. No one knew how many, or where they had come from. The news anchor was calling South Mumbai a warzone. Seconds blurred into minutes that turned into hours. My eyes scanned the news for Pappa. All I knew was that he had gone to CST.

Mummy couldn't bear the anxiety any longer. She began pressing buttons on her Nokia mobile.

'I'm on the spot now,' Pappa said, angrily, as soon as he picked up and then quickly hung up before she could ask any further questions.

The landline rang.

I rushed to the passageway outside the front door to pick it up, but my mother had already grabbed the connecting line in her bedroom.

'Hello?' she said.

It was Darshan, my college friend.

'Hello, *Kaku*. It's Aakash's friend,' he said. 'We can hear gunshots from our home.'

My stomach clenched.

Darshan didn't live anywhere near South Mumbai. He lived midtown, far from the attack site.

'Do you know if we are safe?' he asked. 'We're very worried.'

'I don't know either,' my mother said. 'I hope so.'

This phone call, and Pappa picking up, had brought an air of normalcy to the proceedings. The reporters outside CST made it seem like things were under control. How else was it possible for them to be present near a terrorist attack? Watching live reports of Pappa going to where bullets were being fired brought a curious mix of disbelief, anxiety, and a calm that always seems to accompany high-pressure situations for me. I had realized then that the TV is unable to ever simulate the real stakes of a news event. As long as your surroundings are relatively comfortable, it is very difficult to get a true picture of what is happening. It almost seemed pointless to watch what was unfolding except for the desire to know that Pappa was safe.

Around 1 a.m., as per court records, the TV screen flashed the news that Mummy and I both stared at for a while without saying anything to one another. 'It's not true,' Mummy said eventually, staring ahead with glassy eyes in her maroon nightgown, a treasured possession for decades.

This was my first real experience of death. Mummy's father had died when she was twenty, before I was born. We used Mysore Sandal Soap for most of my childhood because the smell reminded her of her father, a fact that was revealed to me by S, who once found our mother crying by herself in the bedroom while turning a bar of soap in her hand. When S asked her why, my mother replied, 'Because today was the day my father had died.'

Pappa's father, or *Ajoba*, had died in Pune in 2001 or in '02, while we were in Vienna, and his mother, or Nagpur *Aaji*, had died in Nashik in 2006 while we were in Mumbai. The only time I saw Pappa overcome by emotion was when he got the phone calls telling him his parents had died. I had hardly been close to any of my grandparents, and their passing had registered more as a fact than a feeling.

This time, there was a strange, unnerving lump at the bottom of my belly. A deep, intense feeling that soaked through everything I was doing, but somehow remained out of my grasp. As if I had forgotten something very important and was unable to remember it, however hard I tried.

Just a few hours before that news flash, Pappa had been dodging Bruno's nips near the kitchen door. That normal, ordinary moment, the last one, felt almost like a false memory. Twelve hours before the news announced his death, Mummy and Pappa had been talking about whether there were enough idlis for a second helping.

Three days before 26 November, we had celebrated their anniversary at the Cricket Club of India, where Pappa had a service membership. Just the three of us. Something they never did. Something my mother later thanked me for forcing them to do.

Back then, the presence of these memories and the knowledge that Pappa might no longer exist always seemed strangely surreal. Now, since there is no one around who is alive to confirm that these memories ever took place, they almost seem imagined. As if they are part of a movie I had seen long ago and mostly forgotten.

The landline had rung again.

My mother had answered.

'The police are sending a car to take me to the hospital,' she had said, after hanging up.

'I'll come too,' I had said.

'No, you won't.'

'Why not? I want to know what's happening.'

'I don't know if my husband is dead or alive. I can't let anything happen to you too.' She had snapped. 'I won't be able to bear it.'

'What can happen to me inside a police van?' I had yelled back.

'Please. Just stay home.' She had yelled even more loudly.

I gave up. We didn't say anything more. I was the youngest, not just in my own family but on both sides of it. The last remaining child, still to become an adult.

Mummy went in and changed into a salwar kameez, then sat before me waiting for the car to arrive. We didn't say anything to one another about Pappa. I didn't know what she was thinking, nor what one says in moments like these. Her eyes brimmed with tears. The phone rang a few times, but we didn't pick up. Eventually, a blue-and-white Toyota Qualis with a flashing red beacon pulled up. The wrought-iron door outside screeched open. Mummy got up, our plywood front door clicked shut behind her, and the police siren wailed into that hostile Mumbai night as they set off towards the hospital to confirm what no one wanted confirmed.

The rest of that night, and many days after, always return

to me as a series of flashing images: Mummy whose identity for the remainder of her life would be reduced to 'Widow of Slain Martyr Hemant Karkare,' her brown eyes behind gold-rimmed glasses scrunched up in fear; the shifting silhouettes of trees on the windshield of Kiran Mama's Hyundai i10 as we drove to JJ Hospital a few hours after Mummy had left; the harsh fluorescence of the white tube lights in the waiting room at JJ Hospital; the house filling with relatives and distant family friends that I have not seen or met since; a photographer's arm sneaking above the boundary wall, holding an HDV camera trying to capture a shot of Pappa's dead body; the still image of Ajmal Kasab, one of the ten terrorists who laid siege to Mumbai, at Chhatrapati Shivaji Terminus in a black T-shirt and an AK-47 slung over his shoulder.

And then, the clip played on loop on TV channels that night, and for days and years after: Pappa, in his light-blue shirt and black trousers, taking a call on his BlackBerry, hurriedly donning an ill-fitting bulletproof vest and a riot helmet, before rushing off-screen to the right.

The last time I saw him alive.

The distance that had always existed between us continued into his death.

2

You are your own mother and father

Except for during my childhood, I mostly did not have a relationship with my parents. At seventeen, I was not even sure if I liked my parents or if they liked me. Like most Indian families, we weren't the kind to ever hug, say 'I love you,' or show any kind of emotion. I was born in 1991, ten years after my oldest sister and six years after my middle one, when my parents were already in their mid-thirties and had little energy left to care.

For most of my life, I was okay with this non-relationship. One of my clearest childhood memories is from 2nd standard. It was Sports Day in school and the buses were cancelled. My parents were supposed to send someone to pick me up, but no one came. I spent the whole day crying by the gates because they had forgotten.

That, in a sense, was the metaphor for my relationship with my parents. I waited for them to notice me. They didn't. And I picked up the pieces and moved on. Eventually I got used to it, telling myself, *you are your own mother and father.*

As a child, I often thought about a photograph taken of a family vacation before I was born. Pappa in a yellow vest, standing at the bow of a boat on a river, his thinning hair blown back by the wind, his relaxed demeanour making him look impossibly young. Mummy and my sisters sitting on either side of him. All of them at ease in each other's company. It seemed to belong to a different version of the family than the one I had grown up in.

When I asked my sisters how it was possible that they'd once gone on a vacation together as a family, they reworked the classic older-sibling adoption joke and said, 'We were a happier family before you were born.'

I'd go rushing to Mummy for reassurance that this was not true, but I could never really shake off the feeling that my sisters were being more honest than my mother was. For, by the time I was old enough to form memories of family life, what I remember are the non-stop arguments, thunderous in their intensity, full of things no one should ever say to each other, moving from room to room, and usually ending with locked bedrooms and a slammed front door.

My first memories of home and family life also took place in European Quarters, where we were living in 2008. We had first moved there in 1995, when I was four. Back then, we lived on the first floor of the building, directly above the ground-floor flat we would eventually move into.

I remember being afraid of a huge bathroom to the right of the home. There was a beehive outside the window and I often saw spiders jump from the leaves to the windowsill of our bathroom. I was terrified of insects, and my phobia was not helped by the fact that my sisters were completely unafraid of creepy-crawlies and chased me around the home holding cockroaches by their antennas.

One day S and I had discovered a pair of cooing baby pigeons in a crevice by the window of that bathroom. We took the nest down to look at the birds more closely and then kept it back. By the next morning, there was a strong smell of rot. The chicks were dead; their eyes had been pierced through.

It was my first lesson in the brutality of nature. My father, with the grim smile of someone who found macabre stories amusing, explained, 'She thought they were traitors. Imposters. You handled them, and they smelled like humans. That's why you don't mess with the natural world.'

Years later, when I watched the films of Werner Herzog, I

felt like he and Pappa shared a similar outlook towards life and I established Herzog as a kind of father figure in my head.

The balcony of that home overlooked the main road, and sometimes S, a friend, and I would throw ice at unsuspecting passersby, then press ourselves down to the ground beneath flowerpots. For a while, we took great joy in this delinquent behaviour, until one passerby figured it out, rang the doorbell to our house, and complained to Mummy, who told Pappa. He gave us a dressing down for the ages. For once, I couldn't be righteously indignant about his yelling because I knew we were in the wrong. To this day, I feel ashamed of that incident.

Before moving to European Quarters, we had lived in Bhiwandi for nine months, and in Thane for a little over a year before that. Each move was accompanied by my tears at having to leave behind building friends I could have spent long hours playing with. S and J might have gotten used to the moving by then, as I don't recall them having similar teary farewells.

Before Thane, we had lived in Chandrapur. According to a story Pappa once told at a gathering celebrating his twenty-five years in the police force, Mummy had taken me there a week after I was born. I have no memories of our time there, but my sisters always recall it with great fondness. Mummy, however, recalled it as a time when Pappa, for reasons I never discovered, lost interest in home life. She often said, during arguments with him or when upset with us, that she had become a single parent.

And even before that, there was Bhusawal, where S had been born. At some point, I discovered they had also lived in VP Road in South Mumbai, and later in Andheri. Pappa had worked at Hindustan Unilever before he got his government job, and Mummy often liked to joke that we would have been far richer if only he had stayed in the private sector.

In interviews that followed his death, she often said that perhaps Pappa would still be alive if he'd never joined the public sector.

These moves, all part of Pappa's job with postings that changed every few years, meant new schools, new homes, and worst of all for a shy kid like me, the struggle to make new friends. It didn't matter that Pappa had been posted in the Economic Offences Wing or the Narcotics Bureau, because all I really knew about his job then was that he was an IPS officer. This meant a red beacon on his car and a lot of people falling over themselves to salute him and be subservient. Occasionally, a call would make him stand up straight, and he'd keep saying 'Sir, Sir' to an unknown voice on the phone. I'd always wonder what kind of person could have that kind of effect on my father.

These stories of our past lives often reached me through eavesdropped conversations on the rare occasions when we ate together as a family, my parents and sisters laughing about a memory I had no part in. Sometimes, it felt like I was a family of one in this other family of four.

On most days, Pappa existed in fragments at home: long silences, sudden yelling, nothing in between. He was always working, or getting ready for work. Most mornings, he was up by 7 a.m. and out of the door before I even woke up for school.

My heart would sink of its own accord as soon as the clock struck 7.30 p.m., time for Pappa to come home. My parents' arguments could begin with the most innocuous of things: crumbs from the *khari* Mummy dipped into her endless cups of chai that she drank throughout the day left scattered on the counter, spiralling into all the ways they had wronged each other over the years.

These happened in the car on the way home from a get-together, in the middle of the night after everyone had gone to sleep, on the phone at work, and then again at home when everyone was around. Threats of divorce were commonplace. The decibels often reached ear-shattering levels. There was never a resolution, never the kind of reconciliation you see in movies. The bitterness seemed endless.

They would yell at the top of their voices at home and whisper menacingly in public. I'd cower in corners most of the time, and at other times, I'd try to look as innocent and childlike as possible so they would feel guilty and stop fighting, but they almost never did. Pappa would eventually give us a withering look of disgust before walking out of the door. I was always afraid he might get tired of us and never return.

Mummy would cry after these arguments, and sometimes I'd lie down next to her in her arms, afraid of the day I'd be too old for such a thing to be socially acceptable. For that would be the day Mummy would be truly old. The day that she would begin to die.

Sometimes, I'd be sitting in a room and feel Pappa's eyes on me from the doorway, a shiver running down my spine. I was never comfortable in his presence. It felt like I was holding my breath whenever he was around, only safe from his temper at school or outside with friends. I never quite figured out why my family had arranged itself in this way. As I grew older, I got used to this daily occurrence. Less frightened, but the atmosphere at home was like being constantly underwater, unable to breathe clearly.

Due to my deathly fear of Pappa and his temper, I was closer to Mummy. She handled most of the domestic affairs—school, food, extracurricular activities, and since her job ended at 4 p.m., around the time I came back from school, we spent a lot of time together. She spent long hours trying to teach me to read. Our bedroom walls were covered with little pieces of chart paper with words on them. I had to read them aloud, spell them correctly without looking, and eventually, one day I succeeded. She read to me every night, stories of kittens and their mittens, crooked men living in crooked houses. I started loving books. I read to my heart's content.

Most of my memories of Mummy, however, are from after I turned seven or eight, when the tensions in my parents' marriage seemed to drain her. She began to lose interest in her kids, retreating into religion, a refuge it seemed most of her friends who didn't get along with their husbands also sought. I don't remember the good moments anymore, only the bitter things she'd say. As a child, this bitterness reduced my guilt for having checked out of my family life. These days, I just try not to think about it.

My strongest emotion as a child toward my parents was pure shame. I didn't want any of my friends to know how much they argued and how abnormal we seemed as a family. We could scarcely spend any time together without a huge blow-up. So as soon as I made new friends in the new place we had moved to, I tried to spend as much time as possible outside the house.

In European Quarters, my closest friends were the children of the domestic staff who lived in the servants' quarters, on the terrace and in the courtyard behind the building, and worked in the homes of the eight families that lived there. I only learned much later, when I was twelve or thirteen and S was studying decolonization theory for her B.A. at St. Xavier's, why it was called European Quarters. The building had once housed English officers during the British Raj. 'The brown sahib has replaced the white sahib,' S had said once, and we both had laughed.

As soon as I came home from school, I would throw off my bag and go running to the compound outside European Quarters—where, years later, my father's dead body would one day lie on a stage—and play cricket until it was too dark to see the ball. On weekends, we walked hand in hand around the neighbourhood, sometimes even daring to cross the main road outside my home, strictly forbidden by my mother, to knock raw mangoes off the tall trees near the Railway Police Quarters. Occasionally, I'd swipe a fifty-rupee note left lying around the house, and the four or five of us would gorge on *samosa pav* and a *vada pav* each.

My mother was perpetually afraid that my friends would

lead me astray. Cousins, uncles and aunts often asked if it was true that I played with the 'children of maidservants', as though it were the most shameful thing in the world. Even though I knew I was doing nothing wrong, I would vigorously shake my head and try to change the subject. Somewhere in that experience lay my first awareness that who I really was seemed unacceptable to the wider world. To avoid judgement, it was best to keep the real self hidden.

'I used to follow you around,' Mummy told me once, years later. 'I thought those kids would turn you into a smoker. But then I realized they were actually a good influence. All you did was play cricket for long hours. That's why you began to love sports. Pappa was never good at them, which is why he got second rank in the IPS academy instead of first.

'If you'd become friends with the spoiled rich kids you went to school with, there would've been a greater chance of smoking and drinking, because then you'd have had money.'

European Quarters marked the last stable period of my childhood, at least in terms of geography. After three years in Dadar, just as I was finally comfortable with a steady gang of school friends and neighbourhood friends, we had to move again when Pappa was posted to a new department.

3

Losing my mother tongue

Early on in my parents' marriage, maybe even during their courtship, though I can't say for sure, Mummy and Pappa were on a date. That in itself is something I can hardly believe. The two of them found themselves on Marine Drive. In my mind, I borrow scenes from the romantic comedy *Chhoti Si Baat* (1975), with Amol Palekar and Vidya Sinha, to imagine this moment. Bell bottom pants, colourful sarees, the whole frame tinted with sepia. It was here that my father, a railway guard's son from Nagpur, pointed to the houses on Nepean Sea Road, the most expensive real estate in the city, and as the story goes, is claimed to have declared, 'One day, I will have a house there, I will live in one of those buildings.'

'It was this confidence that I loved most about him,' my mother once told me when I asked her what she liked best about my father. 'He believed that if you wanted something, there was nothing stopping you from getting it.'

Pappa's dream came true in 1998. When I was seven, we moved into government quarters on Nepean Sea Road. We had left behind Dadar in Central Mumbai, my mother's favourite place in the whole world, a haven for the 'clerk class', for the posh, manicured streets of South Mumbai, the land of old money and the old rich. For Pappa—who had studied for the UPSC on bus rides from work, borrowed books he couldn't afford from a kindly economics professor, and grown up so poor that his family sometimes alternated between eating and using electricity—this was everything he had been working towards all his life.

In our new home, I encountered, for the first time, children who were rich and always had been that way. Their world was filled with cars and vacations every summer. Their houses had washing machines and microwaves, luxuries in the nineties. They made popcorn at birthday parties, owned the latest computer games that my parents would never buy for me, wore G-shock watches. They spoke exclusively in English, and studied in ICSE schools, where reading Shakespeare was seen as the mark of being truly worldly.

It was a far cry from the schools I had attended until then, where Hindi was the lingua franca and nobody owned anything particularly fancy. Over time, in Nepean Sea Road, I, too, became like the kids around me. My broken English fixed itself. Today, I can hardly recall a time when it did not occupy a central position in my life. Marathi slowly slipped away from being the language in which I thought and spoke with my family, to one I rarely used at all.

I read in English, spoke it with my siblings, and eventually even my parents, who, reluctantly at first, made the transition to keep up with us. One day, when I told my mother that I thought in English, and most likely dreamt in the language too, she was first disbelieving and then dismayed. She mourned the loss of my mother tongue. My father had wanted to put me in a Marathi-medium school. He argued with Mummy that he had turned out fine in one, so why not me? English medium, he said, was pointless. I never found a chance to ask him why. Maybe there was a political reason behind it. His father had been a member of the Communist Party, imprisoned for union strikes. Maybe it was ideological, the belief, common in traditional Indian families, that English-medium schools produced soft, spoiled children who couldn't survive the real world, much like how studying literature or the humanities is dismissed as impractical.

Nepean Sea Road, I think, is what caused the real schism in my relationship with Mummy and Pappa—after which there never seemed like there would be a possibility of a reconciliation.

My parents spoke and thought in Marathi; I, in English. Our frames of reference for each other grew further apart. Their idea of being a good son was not mine, and my idea of good parenting never crossed their minds.

When I was younger, communication with my mother was easier. In Marathi, I used the informal pronoun '*tu*' to address her, felt comfortable holding her hands, or burying my face in her saree when I was embarrassed in public. With my father, it was different. It was always the formal '*tumhi*', always a distance that could never be bridged.

In Nepean Sea Road, our differences with the other families became starker. Most of the other officers had IAS or IPS backgrounds spanning generations. They were connected to celebrities and film stars. Their homes had modern furniture, gleaming white walls without a single chip of paint, like something out of a TV ad. And, most of all, my friends seemed to genuinely enjoy spending time with their parents. They had long lunches on weekends, regular dinners at restaurants, family trips. I would always wait to be invited into their homes just to glimpse what a family could be like. And then, when I returned to ours, I'd see Pappa's black leather shoes by the cabinet and walk slowly into the living room, hoping against hope it was one of those rare nights when there would be peace.

In 2000, Pappa moved to Delhi to begin training for a diplomatic posting under the Research and Analysis Wing (RAW). My sisters and I were instructed not to tell anyone that he was now working for the secret service. I instantly thought of James Bond and spies and became terrified that Pappa's life was in danger. I may have let it slip to one or two friends that he was a spy, but they dismissed it, thinking that it was all made up. By the end of that year, Pappa left for Vienna. My best friend at the time, who seemed to live in a family straight out of a McDonald's commercial, asked me, 'How can you let your father go so far away? I would never allow mine to do that.'

It hadn't even occurred to me to miss Pappa. My sister S and I spoke of it only in terms of relief, a six-month reprieve from his temper, his constant discipline. When I told S about how absurd my friend was being about the whole affair, we laughed. But she replied quietly, 'You do know that some people like spending time with their fathers and love them, don't you? Not all families are like ours.'

Back then, all I could think was that there would be no more nightly fights with Mummy or the endless scoldings about how worthless we were as children and human beings. The reprieve, however, lasted only until the middle of 2001, when my school year ended and S, Mummy, and I travelled to Vienna to begin studying there, so that Pappa could maintain the backstory of a family life while he gathered intelligence for RAW.

As luck would have it, even after a month and a half of trying (and delaying the start of my school term in India), I was unable to secure admission into Vienna International School, where all the diplomats' children went. So I returned to Mumbai, deeply embarrassed, as though I had failed at something, and began studying in the 5th standard again.

By September 2001, I was back in Vienna with an admission into the school, but all of it was against my wishes. I had been happy in India and only lonely in Vienna. Who was going to listen to a ten-year-old whose greatest desire in the world was to play cricket with his friends until he couldn't play anymore, or spend long hours in the well-stocked St. Mary's library, working his way through Enid Blyton's entire back catalogue?

By January 2002, I was back in St. Mary's for the third term. Mummy hadn't adjusted to Vienna and was convinced that 'white people' would have a negative influence on her children. One son of a prominent Indian diplomat had become a DJ, and several others had boyfriends and girlfriends: proof enough, in her mind, that her children would be doomed if they spent any more time in Austria.

'You're treating me like an airplane!' I once yelled at Mummy.

'Don't yell at me. Have the guts to yell at your father,' she had replied, as she often did whenever I accused her of something. And I said nothing further because Pappa would never listen, and I was too afraid of him to protest against anything he did.

Vienna also carries with it a peculiar memory I've never been able to make sense of. One night, while I buried my face in a pillow and pretended to sleep, Pappa ran his hand through my hair and whispered, 'I love you.'

Something that had never happened before, or since.

I hadn't believed the words. Not long before, he had yelled at me in front of a house full of guests because I had accidentally shorted a plug in our old house near Schönbrunn Gardens during a party. I loved tinkering with gadgets, pulling them apart, experimenting with wires and plugs. But this tendency had been labelled 'destructive mentality' by one of Pappa's friends, and from then on, whenever I touched anything, my parents assumed I was doing so only to break it.

That night, he had tried to hit me, but I had slipped away and locked myself in another room. So when he whispered, 'I love you,' I assumed it was guilt on his part, not real. Or maybe I was too puzzled, too embarrassed, to respond. By morning, I thought I had dreamt the entire event.

It's one of those moments that has always come back to me in the years since his death. I've never been able to decide whether it's a sweet memory or tainted with menace, like most of my childhood. Other times, I feel guilt. Was there some possibility of reconciliation on that night?

Pappa's and Mummy's constant fights, the endless moving between countries and houses, eventually led to me being sent to a boarding school in Panchgani in the 6th standard, supposedly for stability. The reason was never fully clear to me, but S explained it later in a letter: 'Pappa didn't trust Mummy to give you the discipline he thought you needed. And he knew you didn't want to live with him in Vienna. So he thought boarding school was a nice middle ground.'

At midterm, when Mummy came to visit me, my housemaster asked her, 'Do you and your husband not get along?'

I went red with shame, my ears burning hot. Mummy smiled awkwardly.

'I only ask because Aakash is a very innocent boy. Sanjivan is like a basket of bad oranges. All these boys come from broken families. If you keep him here too long, he will become a bad orange too.'

And yet, amongst the so-called misfits of boarding school, I felt a strange kind of belonging. It peeled back the false veneer of Indian society, exposing the hypocrisies of the Indian family set-up. Many boys there had been abandoned by their parents, because of divorce, second marriages, or simply because their parents did not want them. Oddly, I felt comfortable amongst them. The only thing I hated was being in school all day, always under authority.

By the end of the year, I pleaded with Mummy to let me return home, and thankfully she agreed. The fees, one lakh a month compared to just a few thousand in Mumbai, surely tilted the decision as well.

Still, one memory of boarding school always stays with me. When I asked Pappa if I could leave, he began writing me faxes filled with advice about the sacrifices one must make in life to become a great man. He once opened a letter with the line: 'I know you miss your mother. Perhaps, even me?'

And then he signed off: *Yours sincerely*.

That puzzled me deeply as a child. Our English teacher had drilled into us the chief difference between a formal letter and informal family letters. You signed off 'Yours sincerely' in a business letter; you signed off 'With love' to your family.

My eyes then, and my mind today, always focus on that phrase 'perhaps, even me?'

What did he think of our relationship? If he knew it was strained, why didn't he try to repair it? At thirty-three, I think maybe he just didn't know how to. S once told me: 'When a man doesn't like his wife, he doesn't like the children he has with her.' At fourteen, I thought it cold and brutal. Now, I think it was at least thirty per cent true.

In 2004, I returned to St Mary's for my 7th standard. I was excited to go back. Living on Nepean Sea Road and studying there had been amongst the happiest memories of my childhood. I couldn't wait to see my friends, play hand cricket at lunch, and argue about Pokemon cards and WWE on the bus rides to school. But something seemed different.

In primary school, uniforms had blurred class differences. There were tiny indications, of course, that some students were wealthier because they arrived in school in chauffeur-driven cars, carrying branded schoolbags, water bottles, and pencil boxes with hidden compartments, their stationery imported from names like Faber-Castell and Staedtler instead of my humble Nataraj. This time, however, it seemed like my friends had changed. They had become meaner in some way. Money had become more important.

My bench partner once called me at home and my mother picked up, which I found out the next day during recess, because he asked: 'Is your mom illiterate?'

'What?'

'Man, she can't even speak English.'

I can still recall the shame that hit me that instant, like a secret I hadn't even realized I was keeping, or was aware of, but now that it was out in the open for all to see, I could feel mortification crawling inside of me.

I cannot remember what I said then. Maybe I got angry, yelled, but I remember him laughing, looking larger than me, even though I was taller.

For years, the taunt festered. I fantasized about showing up at his home, knocking his door, and yelling: 'At least my mother works and earns a living, unlike yours, who only spends your father's money and does your homework.' That's what I should have said. Instead, my shame became his weapon. He held it over me, threatening to tell everyone unless I placated him. And so for the rest of that academic year, I spent my lunch money buying him samosas and Pepsi. Anything to keep my classmates from learning that my mother spoke broken English, greeting people with 'Gud Maarning' instead of the polished version other mothers would use.

That same year, when I was twelve, I was invited to a birthday party at Willingdon Club, a golf club, no less. I was thrilled. My first real party with the cool kids. I would finally see behind another set of tall Mumbai walls.

I always dreamt of entering every part of the city, every closed-off home and compound, just to see what life looked like inside. To discover if it was better than mine, and if it was, how I could claim it. But the party itself was a disappointment. The boys split into two tables, cool kids and uncool kids, and I didn't belong at either.

When it ended, they all left in their fancy cars. I waited in the parking lot, trying to be invisible, until they were gone. I had no car. I was going to take the bus.

'What, Aakash, you don't have a car?' The same boy asked.

'I do have one. The driver is late.'

He waited a while, though his own driver stood ready. But no car came. Eventually, he smirked and left in his Maruti Esteem. 'What a liar you are, Aakash!'

I don't know why I remember these memories so clearly. I can't claim they left lasting wounds. I can't say I was 'bullied' in the conventional sense. I never felt real fear. I was tall, strong, and could probably have beaten the boy up if it came to a physical fight. But sometimes, years later, a walk, a song, or a film would transport me straight back to that year, and the memories came tumbling out. And I can't seem to figure out why they come tumbling out like they do. They feel hermetically sealed, like a perfect work of art. I return to them the way you revisit a favourite movie or book, because each time something new reveals itself. About me. About my family. About the time I grew up in. About my generation. As if those memories hold a mystery, and if I examine them long enough, some great truth will finally reveal itself.

My parents, too, seemed to occupy a similar position. They never looked or spoke like the parents of other children. They, too, always seemed ill at ease. Outwardly, they belonged to the world of the upwardly mobile group of Indians, but my father had broken out of his lower middle-class childhood. Once, when I told him a friend had remarked that our house looked 'old-fashioned', he snapped, 'Should I take bribes like his father?'

I would watch my friends' parents arrive in fancy cars, beautiful mothers, fair-skinned, in Ray-Bans, their English polished to perfection. By contrast, our home, with its analogue television and years-old sofa, looked decidedly 'old-fashioned', just as my friend had said.

At school, I often got poor marks on projects. Other kids scored higher because their mothers practically did the homework for them. My uniform was always too big, because my parents had decided one oversized set would last two years and save money. My shoes were caked in mud, my shirt perpetually crumpled, my hair unkempt, things neither I nor my parents cared about. A clever classmate even coined a rhyme about me: *Aakash Kar-Kar-ay, crumpled shirt every day.*

At St. Mary's, the friends I had once been eager to return to, began to mock me instead. They suggested my parents were divorced, that was why they lived in different countries, and that I was lying about it. Even my school calendar betrayed me: there was no signature under the line marked 'Father.' It felt as though my worst childhood fears had come true, that everyone had discovered my parents didn't get along. When Pappa returned to India a few months later, I forced him to sign the calendar.

'He wants to tell people in school that he has a father,' Mummy said to him. 'Even though it mostly doesn't seem like it.'

Pappa first looked angry, then laughed, and then turned away, embarrassed.

By 2005, I was in the 8th standard, studying once again at Don Bosco, where I had first begun school a decade earlier. We were back in Mummy's favourite place in the world: Dadar TT. 'I was born here and I am going to die here,' she'd often say and guffaw loudly.

Pappa was still in Vienna. His three-year posting stretched to four, then five, then six years. The years of his posting were a difficult time for our family. Without Pappa, Mummy's anxiety and rage only grew. She spent long hours fighting with S and me, berating us about how she had been forced to raise us as a single parent. We didn't know how to respond. Today, I have more sympathy for her than I did as a teenager, but even nostalgia cannot soften the bleakness of some of those childhood moments.

When Pappa was scheduled to return from Vienna, S, Mummy and I sat in her bedroom in the retirement flat my parents had purchased in Dadar's Hindu Colony, voicing our fears about the return of old fights and anger. 'My children have returned to me because our common enemy is going to come back,' Mummy laughed, clapping her hands. It was one of the last times I remember us feeling close.

All the executive decisions they had made on my behalf without consulting me, combined with the stormy home life that never let up, created a wide gulf between us. As a child, I may not have been able to articulate it, but now it seems as though we were only a family because of biology. There were no deeper bonds. Whenever Pappa and Mummy fought and Pappa stormed out, he would look at me weeping and say, 'Don't worry, I'll pay your school fees...that's all you want from me, don't you?'

I never knew how to respond. Maybe part of me felt guilty that this was the only relationship he thought we had. Another part was indignant: what was I supposed to do about it? I was a child; he a grown man, an IPS officer, no less. Today, I simply see them as flawed human beings, thrown into a family life they were not suited for, raising children they never truly wanted, trapped in a marriage that should never have lasted. But Maharashtrian society offered no escape from a life one did not want. Sometimes I think, had they never married, had we three never been born, perhaps they would have been happier. It's a strange realization, to feel that your parents might have led better lives if you had never existed.

Pappa returned in 2006, rejoining the IPS as a Joint Commissioner. After stints in the Administrative Wing and the Anti-Corruption Bureau, he moved to the Anti-Terrorist Squad in 2007 and returned to European Quarters. By then, I had changed schools five times and lived in four different homes. I would boast, pointlessly, but proudly, that I had the unique distinction of having studied in four different school boards: ICSE, CBSE, SSC and IB.

The lives of my former friends had diverged too far from mine. We tried playing cricket together a few times, but we had nothing in common, and soon stopped meeting. All the moves, the secrecy around my parents, and the constant fear of Pappa's temper had made me a shy child. I avoided eye contact, I hardly had any friends, and I spent most of my time immersed in books.

It wasn't until 11th standard that I finally seemed to come out of my shell. For years, I had found it very difficult to reveal anything about myself, haunted by the fear of being judged by external sources. But I did make friends who seemed to understand the parts of me I had always kept hidden.

We rode the top deck of Bus No. 66, letting the wind whip through our hair on the way to CST. We went to Leopold because

Gregory David Roberts's bestseller *Shantaram* had made it famous, though we were too nervous to order beer, so we drank overpriced milkshakes instead. We spent long hours on the low wall outside RA Podar, called the *katta*, bunking lectures, gossiping, laughing, making fun of one another. Since my house was closest to college, and my parents were rarely home, it became our hangout. We'd buy a dozen vada pavs, share them amongst the five of us, and talk endlessly about nothing, teasing each other about our crushes, making plans that never went anywhere. For someone who had spent so long wishing his life were like those in books, I finally felt that life was good.

Even Mummy and Pappa seemed to argue less. When I mentioned this years later, after Pappa's death, Mummy corrected me: 'You're wrong. We were fighting more than ever then.' Maybe I had simply grown numb to it after seventeen years; it had become my normal.

The three of us lived together like uneasy roommates, each leading our own lives. Mummy was absorbed in her work as a college professor and her religious pursuits, 'Art of Living', Chinmaya Mission. Pappa had his job and his friends, his absence after work the constant trigger for my parents' arguments.

I had resigned myself to stop caring about them. My only goal was to get a job that paid well enough to let me leave, to never again live in an unhappy home, never tiptoe around in fear, never feel unsafe. I wanted to live life on my own terms, to do as I pleased. Like most seventeen-year-olds, I believed escape was the only way forward. I didn't know if I would ever speak to Mummy and Pappa again after I left.

4

The spectacle of funerals

It's often said that funerals are more for the living than they are for the dead, which feels like stating the obvious. Even if the afterlife were to exist, I doubt spirits linger near their pyres to ensure rituals and protocols are followed. I am unsure what the burning of human flesh on wood is supposed to achieve, or the point of communal weeping in public, or half-naked priests chanting in Sanskrit. None of these customs lessen the burden of death, nor do they offer any solace or meaning, at least not to me. Perhaps they do for the devout, though even then, I remain unconvinced. In Pappa's case, the funeral had been turned into a spectacle. And Mummy, my sisters and I seemed to have become unwilling participants inside a play.

In the days after Pappa's death, I drifted through the many rooms in our apartment, numb and confused. I didn't want all the people who had gathered there, yet I lacked the power to stop them. Added to my non-existent relationship with Pappa, his strained marriage with Mummy, and the bitter memories of my childhood, I now carried a new burden: a public outpouring of grief, political controversy, and a father who, in death, had been claimed by the outside world.

For days, I scoured newspapers and obituaries, desperate for details, clues, fragments of Pappa. I wanted to uncover who the man who had been my father for seventeen years really was. His identity became a mystery I needed to solve, and I cast myself as a detective.

'His colleagues say he was always calm and composed.' [2]

'Normally, it is almost impossible to find a chief of the Anti-Terror Squad quoting lines from Tagore's Geetanjali *in casual discussions. But Hemant Karkare, who fell to terrorists' bullets on Wednesday night, was an unusual man. A well-read, learned, and multi-faceted police officer, he stood apart in the force.'*

Born in Jabalpur, Karkare finished his engineering from Nagpur before joining a private firm. 'All my college friends are in very good positions today, probably earning a zero more than me,' he would say. 'But I am sure none of them have had the experiences I have had.'

Karkare had taken over as ATS chief by choice, leading investigations into the Malegaon blasts and dismantling several terror modules. Before this, he headed the administration wing of the Mumbai Police and played a crucial role in its modernization efforts.

But perhaps his most coveted posting was his nine-year stint with India's external intelligence agency, the Research and Analysis Wing (RAW). He preferred to call it a posting with the Cabinet Secretariat and spent years stationed at the Indian mission in Vienna.

Nine years? Hadn't he been posted there for five? Or six, at most?

Did he *like* to call it a posting with the Cabinet Secretariat? Or had he been told to? Wasn't it officially described as a Ministry of External Affairs posting, a cover story to conceal his role with RAW?

Did he really say those things about his friends earning more than him? I'd never heard him say such a thing. Not only were the newspapers getting things wrong, but they were also wholly inadequate at revealing the person beyond the biographical details.

---

[2]Agashe, Ashish, 'The memories of Black Wednesday', *economictimes.indiatimes.com*, 28 November 2008, https://tinyurl.com/3hdmr3ma. Accessed on 16 December 2024.

> Maharashtra Anti-Terrorism Squad (ATS) chief Hemant Karkare, who was probing the Malegaon blasts case, suffered three bullet injuries to his chest while leading the offensive against the terrorists in one of their hideouts early that morning.[3]
>
> One of the officers in the force, Karkare had solved the serial bomb blasts in Thane, Vashi, and Panvel. He was also credited with the groundbreaking revelations in the September 29 Malegaon blast investigation. Known for his discipline and fairness, he instructed his officers never to create false evidence, reminding them: 'We should do our job, and it is for the court to decide.'
>
> In his final interview to a television channel yesterday, he referred to getting the custody of Malegaon blast accused Sadhvi Pragya Singh Thakur, and said 'police custody would have helped investigations to proceed faster but still we will see how best to deal with it in a legal way.'

I didn't know what to do with this information about his professional life at 17. It somehow felt less important by comparison than what was happening inside our home. The most alienating bit of those profiles was their attempt to paint us as a perfect family. Mummy and Pappa as the perfect parents, in a perfect marriage, raising their children lovingly for three decades. Until then, I'd never realized that the news could be wrong. I began to sense that something intangible lingered around an event, something only those inside it could see. What else were they getting wrong? What other lies were being told?

'I never knew Pappa,' I confessed to a cousin.

I whispered it as we sat on the double bed in my room, surrounded by a sea of relatives whose voices drifted in and out like background noise. To say aloud the thought I had first

---

[3]*PTI*, 'ATS chief Hemant Karkare dies a hero's death', *economictimes.indiatimes.com*, 27 November 2008, https://tinyurl.com/4muj7c82. Accessed on 16 December 2024.

formed in the bathroom of JJ Hospital felt almost shameful, as though I'd committed a cardinal sin. As though I were Meursault the protagonist of Albert Camus's *The Stranger*, one of Pappa's favourite novels, sipping tea with milk on the day of my mother's funeral. I feared a relative might overhear and snap, *How dare you say that about a hero?*

'Who said?' My cousin replied, her response strangely flat against what felt like a monumental revelation to me.

But in those early days, everyone seemed to be saying something. A woman none of us knew walked into our home and declared, 'The RSS killed your father.'

We received hate mail signed by someone calling herself '*Sadhvi*', a word I didn't know then, but later learned meant the female counterpart of Sadhu, someone who supposedly lived in an ashram and prayed all day. That didn't strike me as leaving much time for writing hate letters. I even drafted a reply in my scrawny handwriting, the same handwriting my parents always despised, and asked my father's constable, Sachin, to post it for me. But the sender's address was incomplete, so it never left the house

In the papers, my kaku was suddenly my mother. My cousin became my father's only daughter. S, who was doing her master's in Germany, was said to be pursuing a PhD in the UK. I was listed as a B.Com. student when I was still in 12th standard. The number of terrorists kept shifting—twenty, then twelve, when in fact there were only ten. The culprits changed names too: first Indian Mujahideen, then Deccan Mujahideen, then Lashkar-e-Taiba. They had come from within India, then from Britain, then the US, then Pakistan.

Even official reports contradicted one another. They couldn't agree on how many bullets had struck Pappa, or why his bulletproof jacket had failed. Just months before his death, several right-wing politicians had criticized him; now, those same voices rushed to celebrate his bravery. It was too much information for me to process, and slowly I began to shut the news out.

Mummy asked one of our house helps, Sangeeta, to cut out every article about Pappa and paste them into a file. I didn't open that file then, nor in the many years it gathered dust in the storeroom. These days, I think it has been lost to the ether.

'I'm saying it,' I eventually told my cousin. 'We hardly ever spoke.'

'Oh, okay,' she replied, unsure how else to respond. 'It's okay. It's fine.'

I told her about a conversation between two characters in the animated film *Waking Life* (2001). How the brain stays awake for a few minutes after death, and how, in that suspended time, those minutes stretch into an eternity. Like when you wake up in the morning, glance at the clock, 8 a.m., then drift back to sleep. It feels like you've been sleeping forever, but when you check again, only three minutes have passed.

I hesitated, then asked, 'What do you think Pappa thought about after he died?'

She didn't respond. It wasn't really a question for her; it was for me. I wanted to know he if thought of us. Did he have any regrets? I knew he kept talking about going backpacking across Europe. Or writing a memoir of his own. I wanted Mummy and Pappa to be free of the burden that society, extended family, and relatives seemed to place on them, to lead the lives they wanted. For Pappa, that possibility had been forever snatched away. Was that what he thought in those final moments?

I knew I'd have to wait for S and J to arrive before I could talk about these things. It was an unsayable truth only the three of us shared: how Pappa never really liked being at home, how he spent most of his time at work or with friends, how loudly he yelled at us, how he always knew exactly what to say to make it hurt. His favourite word for us was *dukkar*, pig. Everything was becoming more confusing now that Pappa was being turned into *Hemant Karkare, 26/11 Martyr.*

To me, that was the least interesting part of his identity.

He was just Pappa. I could still see him as a living, breathing figure. I remembered his scent, a mix of colognes and unnamed fragrances, something only he smelled like. How he woke up around the same time every day to do jumping jacks and lift weights for an hour before vigorously rubbing Lacto Calamine lotion onto his skin. How he'd say *'me boltoy'*, (it's me) on the phone after I picked up, as if that was enough. The thumbnail on his right hand curved into a sharp point. His favourite joke: 'What do you call a man who gets diarrhoea after eating too many mangoes?' 'An Amba-ssador.'

J arrived first, then S. We talked about ordinary things, updates about our lives, small observations, and every now and then something about Pappa surfaced. How he said *'unh'* in a particular way. How he could spot dust in any room with supernatural precision. How he once investigated who broke a marble dolphin with the seriousness of a police inquiry. How J remembered him celebrating elaborate birthday parties in Chandrapur. How he was proud of S for earning a full scholarship to study in the UK and Germany.

'I feel like all the conversations I ever had with Pappa would struggle to fill up one of those two-hundred-page Navneet school notebooks,' I told S.

We were sitting in my bedroom, surrounded by relatives, family friends, and several other people I didn't know.

S looked back at me in surprise.

'Well, that's more than I ever spoke to him,' she said. 'Mine would probably be around a hundred pages.'

That was impossible, I thought. S actually spoke to Pappa. I remembered once watching them talk. She asked him, 'Why do you get so angry and yell at everyone?' and he didn't get angry then. He said something thoughtful back. I didn't hear it because I was spying from the living room balcony at Nepean Sea Road. The truth was, I was lying because the real answer seemed too embarrassing.

'If yours is a hundred, then mine won't be more than fifty,' I said. 'I remember you speaking to him a lot more than I ever did.'

'Everyone is sharing happy memories of him,' I told J later, when we had some privacy. 'But I don't seem to have any.'

'Surely, you must,' she replied.

'He taught me to play table tennis when I was ten,' I said.

'There you go, that's a good memory.'

'Well, he yelled and shouted at me so much that I forced myself to learn, just so I wouldn't be yelled at anymore.'

'Well, then at least it's a memory.'

'There's another one, I guess. We were playing Scrabble once,' I continued.

'He never played Scrabble with me,' J replied.

'Yeah, I won the game because I knew how to use the Double and Triple Word scores.'

'That's sweet.'

'I guess. Then I said I won because my vocabulary was better than his. So he got angry and asked Mummy to open the dictionary to any random page. She flipped to 'R', and the first word on the page was 'renege'. I didn't know what it meant, but he did. I guess he memorized the dictionary while preparing for the civil services exam.'

'He was never sure of his English,' S said. 'So, he forced himself to become better.'

The real Pappa only appeared to me in these stories, most of which came from S. Everyone else had turned him into a cartoonish figure out of *Amar Chitra Katha*. The real parts of his persona were stripped away, and he had become a myth in an instant. Since he never really opened up to anyone or said what was on his mind, he became a blank canvas upon which relatives, family friends, the media, and politicians could paint whatever patterns suited their narrative.

'One Sunday, years ago, Pappa drove us to Metro Cinema,'

I said. 'There was no driver. We got a haircut there and then came home.'

'See, that's a happy memory,' J said.

She seemed to hold the warmest memories of my father, or maybe she was just more pragmatic and forgiving.

'Is it, though, or is it just a memory?' I replied. 'A few days ago, Mummy and Pappa fought. They said something…um…'

'What?'

'"I had these kids because of you," Pappa said,' I finally mumbled. 'As if Mummy forced him and he never wanted us.'

'Parents say that,' J replied.

'I've heard much worse,' S added.

'Maybe he didn't love any of us,' I said.

'What's the point of thinking about it?' J replied.

'I think I'm not feeling any grief. Everyone else is crying. Is it weird I'm not?'

Every square inch of the three rooms, hall, kitchen, corridor, passage, was crammed with people. Mummy was locked in the bedroom most of the time, surrounded by a few friends, unable to stop crying, as mourners filed in one by one to pay their respects. Everyone wore solemn expressions. The heaviness of the occasion felt oppressive, bouncing off the faces of visitors, spreading across the ceiling, seeping into the floor, and suffusing the house like vapour. Conversations shrank to hushed tones and whispers.

A couple of my father's friends, men I knew only as 'Uncle', those mysterious adults from gatherings who talked about stock markets and how things were back in their day, tried to hug me. It felt awkward, forced, like something they thought they were supposed to do.

An old man with snowy white hair and a French beard patted my shoulder. 'Your father made the ultimate sacrifice. Be proud, my boy.'

I didn't know how to respond.

I overheard someone whispering: *Wasn't she supposed to wear white? Shouldn't a widow's bangles be broken? How come Kavita was eating achaar?*

I have seldom seen anyone's life improving because of relatives. Indian relatives only seem to exist to provide background commentary and to be as insensitive as possible in the most trying of times.

A distant relative, whose name I can no longer recall, rushed in, a notepad clutched in one hand, scribbling furiously while glancing around looking guilty. She worked as a journalist for a daily.

At some point, she turned to me. 'Do you have a foolscap sheet?'

I wanted to yell at her, to tell her to stop, to ask what exactly do you need to write down? But the words never came. Instead, I nodded, walked to my desk, and tore a double page from one of my college notebooks. She took it without another word and continued scribbling.

Someone else called to ask if passes would be available to see my father's dead body. News reporters and camera crews began to assemble outside the front gate of European Quarters. Next to them, Mumbai residents clad in white stood silently holding candles.

In one room, an elderly uncle who was known to be melodramatic was looking tearfully pleading with a priest who had dropped by, insisting that he should be the one to conduct the funeral. Even though I was an atheist and did not believe in rituals, I told them, 'It's fine, I will do it.'

'Your father would be proud of you,' my uncle said.

That was a strange thing for someone to be proud of. Would Pappa really want to be proud of me for conducting his funeral, or would he simply want to be alive so that no one had to conduct his funeral at all?

I remember a sob breaking through the house. I followed it into the get-together room, Pappa's favourite space, built specially to host parties for his IPS colleagues. Tears streamed down Mathane's face. He was Pappa's rider, the assistant figure who usually sat in the passenger seat of an officer's car. His testimony would later form a large part of the court records.

'He kept asking for help. A bulletproof car. He was standing near JJ Flyover…' he was saying.

For the first time the details of Pappa's death began to take shape in my mind. Blood running down a light-blue shirt. A body left in the street. Over the years, through newspaper articles and books, I kept piecing more together: that Kasab had dragged my father and the other two officers in the vehicle, Ashok Kamte and Vijay Salaskar, out of the Toyota Qualis as they tried to ambush the terrorists at Cama Hospital. That Kasab had fired once again to confirm that they were dead. Thinking about these things has always felt too brutal, too senseless. Even now, it's never easy. On most days, I just bury this information deep into my soul.

By later that morning, the newspapers had begun reporting every tiny detail, sometimes even telling me what I had supposedly been doing.

'Friends came to see him, but son was sleeping,' one headline read.

They also reported how my mother had reacted to my father's death, turning grief into another public spectacle.

'Karkare's wife was initially told that he was injured,' read an article in *Mumbai Mirror*, adding that my mother had rushed to JJ Hospital without waiting for her 'son who studied in a city college.' At the hospital, it said, her blood pressure had shot up and she had collapsed, but she refused to be admitted. Instead, she had chosen to stay outside the room where my father's body was kept.[4]

---

[4]Andhale, Santosh, 'Karkare's wife was initially told that he was injured', *mumbaimirror.indiatimes.com*, 28 November 2008, https://tinyurl.com/48yc828m. Accessed on 16 December 2024.

In the compound outside our home, police vehicles were cleared from the compound, and a stage was being erected. Who was erecting it, and why, I never learned. The relatives overseeing it seemed almost vulgarly attracted to the crowd of cameras. People jostled to bask in the reflected spotlight of Pappa's death. I was furious, and with no one else to confront, I told Mummy, 'Why are you letting them do this? I don't want Pappa's body to be displayed like something in a museum.'

But she did not have the energy to listen. Most of her time was spent shut away in her room, where I heard loud wailing from behind the locked door. I didn't know what to do about it. I was uncomfortable with emotion; she was uncomfortable speaking to me. Perhaps the way we saw the whole affair was fundamentally different. I wanted our family to stare directly at the sun, to use everything exposed by this death to finally confront all the things we had left unresolved. For Mummy, now was the time to focus only on the good.

I was grieving 'Pappa', a parent I had never truly known, now being claimed by the outside world. She was grieving 'Hemant', the man she had loved for over two decades, who had left behind a complicated public legacy that she would have to untangle.

~

Narendra Modi, the then Chief Minister of Gujarat, was scheduled to arrive. My mother had told him not to come three times before, because he belonged to the Bharatiya Janata Party (BJP), which had launched a smear campaign against Pappa in the months leading up to the 2008 attacks.[5]

Modi showed up regardless.

He nodded at me from the stage, folded his hands before my father's body, cameras clicking in rapid succession. Then

---

[5]Hameed, Abdul, 'Karkare family refuses Narendra Modi's financial offer', *twocircles.net*, 30 November 2008, https://tinyurl.com/2jj64tcs. Accessed on 16 December 2024.

he walked into the house. He sat in the living room and later emerged to tell the assembled reporters that he had offered my mother one crore rupees, which she had turned down.

My mother always claimed that conversation never happened.

She hadn't met him at all. And if she had, she would have asked why he had criticized Pappa, and, now that he was here, how he could help us get answers to the questions still haunting her.

Why hadn't the bulletproof jacket worked properly? Why hadn't the Mumbai Police been given better equipment? Revolvers against AK-47s?

This part of the story is always conveniently erased. It is usually retold as: Modi offered help, but Karkare's widow refused him. Or, in a more inspirational tone: Modi offered help, but Karkare's widow refused him because he had criticized her husband.[6]

Neither version is particularly accurate.

For years after 26/11, whenever someone heard my last name, they would ask me about this story. Always with the same angle: the brave widow rejecting hypocritical politicians and their empty offers. Most times, I just nodded along, unwilling to correct them. Some, like my school friends and my tennis coach, would joke that Mummy should have taken the money because one crore was better than no crore. I always laughed awkwardly and swiftly changed the subject. Like Pappa, Mummy too was being turned into a myth, stripped of her humanity in the process. A pawn inside a story other people thought would sell.

Sometimes, I'd go back to an article in *The Telegraph*[7]—the only publication that had reported it correctly, just to make sure I wasn't imagining my own past.

Maharashtra Navnirman Sena's Raj Thackeray too came

---

[6]Staff reporter, 'Hemant's sacrifice should lead to strengthening the country', *rediff.com*, 14 January 2009, https://tinyurl.com/3xtvmvwf. Accessed on 16 December 2024.
[7]TT Bureau, 'When Modi turned up at Karkare's house', *telegraphindia.com*, 20 April 2019, https://tinyurl.com/53nym27e. Accessed on 16 December 2024.

to our house. He, too, sat on the same couch where I had been sitting just days earlier, then left when my mother refused to see him. What political figures hope to achieve by doing this is anybody's guess.

Bruno, the Doberman puppy, was the only one to get solace on that stage.

He had arrived in a crate in the middle of the night a few months ago. 'I got him for you,' Pappa said to me the following morning.

J, S and I had grown up on *The Famous Five*, and George's brown mongrel Timothy had inspired us to beg for a dog of our own on several birthdays. That surprise had never come to pass. Why a dog now when both my sisters had moved out and I had neither the time nor inclination for a pet that needed to be walked twice a day?

Years later, in one of the many conversations I had with strangers after they had learned my surname, the mystery resolved itself.

This time my shoulder was dislocated, and the stranger was a hospital receptionist checking me in for an X-ray.

'Didn't you have a Doberman puppy called Bruno? I remember reading about it in *Loksatta*. Your father got him as protection.'

Bruno hadn't stopped barking since Pappa died. The two of them had shared a bond that surprised us all. Pappa maintained a file of Bruno's medical documents and nursed him back to health when he fell sick.

'He never did that for our Rahu, Ketu and Shanu,' Mummy had said while he pored over the files. She liked to call her three children by those names, the forces of destruction in Hindu mythology.

'Take him to the stage,' the melodramatic uncle suggested while the household, frustrated, watched Bruno barking that morning. Bruno was brought to the stage and quieted down next to Pappa. 'Now he knows his master is dead,' the uncle added.

Did animals miss people? Could they? Or was it just the endless stream of strangers and the chaos stressing Bruno out? He seemed quieter, but I wasn't sure if it was grief or exhaustion.

It was night. The house was still too bright, every single light in the living room switched on. The crowd had thinned. Mummy stayed in her room. J had gone to her in-laws' home in Matunga, away from the madness of a house touched by death. S and I sat in the living room, ignoring the murmuring crowd.

The doorbell rang.

Mathane walked towards me through the curtains at the entrance of the room and handed me a few objects: a gold chain, a sheaf of rupees inside a money clip, and a small black pocket diary. All of them were stained red. The last signs that Pappa had once existed. For reasons I can't explain, I felt compelled to bring them to my nose. They smelled of iron and printed ink.

I flipped through the pages of the diary. 'Lunch' was scheduled for the next day. 'Meeting' for a few days later. The thought that Pappa would no longer be alive to go for that meeting broke me. For the first time, the weight of his death hit me.

Before I could react, a relative plucked the objects from my hands, murmuring over them with interest, like someone admiring artefacts at an art exhibit.

A flash of rage shot through me.

I snatched the diary back and handed everything to Mummy, who locked them in the Godrej steel cupboard in her bedroom. That emotion, rage at intrusion, became a constant in those days. Anytime I tried to think about what had happened, some interruption arrived: the media, a political figure, a distant relative, a family friend. I buried my feelings deep, hoping that maybe in a few weeks I'd be able to process them. I don't know if this rage I felt as a seventeen-year-old ever truly left me.

~

In the early hours of Saturday, 29 November 2008, sustained gunfire was reported inside the Taj Mahal Palace Hotel and Nariman House. The operation was named *Black Tornado*, in which NSG commandos rappelled down from helicopters and flushed out the terrorists. By the time Commissioner of Police Hassan Gafoor declared the siege over, nearly two hundred lives had been lost, three hundred more wounded. Nine terrorists were killed. One was captured. The attack had lasted sixty hours. Finally, it was over.[8]

Pappa's funeral was scheduled for that same morning. His body was brought into the living room and placed on the floor, exactly sixty hours after he had died, in the same spot where our sofa had been, where, just two nights ago, I had sat watching the India-England match.

Mummy burst into tears.

'How could you have let this happen?' she said to Mathane, her voice breaking. 'The police should have been better prepared.'

Mathane had no answer. He just stood there, head bowed, eyes red, the only member of the force who seemed genuinely affected, who showed up and seemed to care.

The body before us wasn't Pappa. His head looked strangely shaped. His eyes were closed. His features seemed alien. I reached out, hesitated, and touched his cheek. Ice cold. Something inside me recoiled.

Pappa was dead. But he had been gone long before this moment.

I had thought this ritual of placing the body in the living room, one I'd seen in countless films, would bring closure. Instead, it felt like sticking a finger deep inside a fresh wound and twisting it. Simple grief wasn't enough. Society seemed to demand a loud, public expression of it.

The actual funeral comes back to me only in flashes. Huge

---

[8]Sanghvi, Vir, *26/11: The Attack on Mumbai*, Penguin Books India, New Delhi, 2009, p. 45.

crowds. More invasive cameras. Tear-streaked faces. Yellow flowers raining down on the truck in which I stood with some members of the police force on the way to the crematorium. I remember walking around the pyre, a *matka,* earthen pot, in my hands, the water refusing to seep out. A relative, and later a friend, remarking, 'I didn't know you were so fat.' The Arabian Sea in the distance. My father's forehead, a blob of ghee at its centre. The 21-gun salute, each shot resounding through the crematorium, knocking ash from the chimney of the electric furnace in my line of view. My mother, aged by decades in a few days. The pyre alight. The smoke from Pappa's burning flesh stinging my eyes as I sat away from the fire, gaze fixed on my feet, trying to forget the world.

I thought of a conversation I once had with Pappa, the summer after my 10th standard. I had made a reading list of Great Books for myself because I wanted to become a man of the world, but also because I knew he had done the same in his school library in Nagpur. I had picked up Ernest Hemingway's classic novel about the Spanish civil war *For Whom the Bell Tolls* because it was one of his favourites, but found it boring. I asked him why he liked it. 'It starts with the title,' he said. 'It's a quote from a poem: "*Therefore, send not to know for whom the bell tolls, it tolls for thee.*"'

I sat in the crematorium, staring at the ground. My nostrils thick with the smell of burning flesh. I tried not to look at the flashing cameras or the reporters talking into microphones. Growing up, I had believed death was one of the most private acts. No one should photograph anyone's dead body. But Pappa had been denied even that privacy.

'Do you know Vandana Kaku?' a woman in white suddenly asked.

'No, I don't,' I said, looking up.

In the background, the flames had engulfed my father's pyre completely. I followed the little curls of black smoke drifting upward until they disappeared into the sun.

'Okay then, do you know Akshata Vahini?' she asked.

'No, I don't.'

'Okay, I am her cousin.'

'Okay,' I said.

'I am a TV reporter. Do you have a bite? How do you feel?'

This moment still plays on loop in my head sometimes whenever I think about those days in November. As we grow older, we accept many things as normal that, as children, we once found deeply abnormal. Some part of the innocence I still carried at seventeen withered away right then. I cannot imagine a normal person asking a child for a sound bite while the smell of burning flesh fills the air at a crematorium. Some humanity is lost forever in such moments, when people refuse to pause and reflect on what they are doing. For years, I remained angry about moments like these. Whenever someone asked me about 'Hemant Karkare' after learning my surname, whenever a journalist tried to reach out, whenever a friend asked with vulgar curiosity what it felt like to be a martyr's son—all I could think about was that one moment. The stench of burning flesh in my nostrils, the woman in white asking me for a 'bite', and the flashing cameras that had turned death into cinema.

Later that day, I saw all that footage played on loop on the TV in our living room, by strangers sitting casually on our couch. Close to 5,000 people had been there.[9]

'Leaders from the saffron alliance, who have been taking potshots at the ATS for targeting Hindu groups in its probe into the October 29 blast at Malegaon, like Manohar Joshi, Nitin Gadkari, and Vinod Tawde were seen at Karkare's funeral at Dadar on Saturday.'[10]

---

[9]Staff reporter, '5,000 attend Hemant Karkare's funeral', *mumbaimirror.indiatimes.com*, 29 November 2008, https://tinyurl.com/3n8snzbs. Accessed on 16 December 2024.

[10]ET Bureau, 'City bids emotional farewell to Karkare', *economictimes.indiatimes.com*, 30 November 2008, https://tinyurl.com/ym8w6d86. Accessed on 16 December 2024.

A shot of me sitting down to cry on the truck was scored by music that could have come straight from an Ekta Kapoor soap. An anchor intoned with manufactured sorrow: *'He used to play in his lap. Now he is lighting his pyre.'*

But this was not the relationship I shared with my father. I didn't want my life turned into a cheesy Bollywood movie. Before I could say anything, S walked into the room, picked up the remote, and switched the TV off.

The screen went black.

Now, I had thought, *we could finally move on.*

5

Terror has no religion

I knew in 2008 that there were controversies involving Pappa's investigation into the Malegaon blasts case. Right-wing Hindutva parties such as the BJP, the Shiv Sena, and the Rashtriya Swayamsevak Sangh (RSS) had criticized him because some of those he arrested and charged with terrorist activities were Hindu. Most of what I knew came in bits and pieces, snippets of breakfast conversations, rare exchanges with Pappa, or a *Mumbai Mirror* headline I skimmed after reading the paper back to front, from celebrity gossip and sports to the political news I usually ignored.

'Terror has no religion,' I remember Pappa telling Mummy during a conversation about work. At the time, I hadn't given it much importance.

A few days before that Wednesday in November, he had an unusual conversation with me about his job.

'How was your day?' he had asked me as I was shuffling awkwardly around my room, trying to make myself scarce, arranging my books and dusting, convinced this was a prelude to a scolding.

'Fine, I studied.'

'All good with your studies?'

Maybe I am in deep trouble, I thought. It had been years since we'd spoken like this.

'Yes,' I replied.

He didn't say anything further, glancing around the room. Sometimes I thought Pappa was as shy and awkward around me as I was around him.

'Have your friends asked anything about me?' he asked.

'No,' I said, then added, 'All my friends are secular.'

The conversation ended there. He went for his nightly walk, as the doctor had prescribed, and I went back to my studies.

At one point, Pappa had even asked if I wanted a bodyguard.

I'd laughed and said no. 'That would mean the terrorists are winning,' I told him.

He'd laughed too, and said nothing more.

In the months since his latest posting, thick black tomes, academic titles with the faces of men in uniform or masks on their covers, had begun piling up on his teakwood bedside table, a permanent fixture in our home. The boundary wall at the edge of European Quarters, separating us from the busy main road, had been raised, and two armed policemen now sat permanently outside our living room window. Newspapers reported these measures, something that had never happened in our life before. Occasionally, friends would ask me questions about Pappa or our home that even I didn't know the answers to.

His work, coupled with a recent diagnosis of diabetes, that sent his blood sugar levels soaring past 350 (normal being around 100), had made him look much frailer and older than I ever remembered him looking. Heavy bags had formed under his eyes, twitching furiously when he spoke. Or perhaps it was simply that I now stood 6 feet 6, half a foot taller than him. The commanding figure who once towered over me, whose eyes I could never meet directly, seemed diminished.

Over the years, many people—journalists, reporters, sometimes even friends and strangers—have asked me about his final days, about what he thought or said. I realized then that people often projected their own family dynamics onto others. If Pappa had been an accountant or held some ordinary job, perhaps he might have spoken freely at the dinner table. But he was a police officer, investigating state secrets. And besides, we hardly ever had dinner together. There was no way for me to know.

The ATS team's investigations had led to arrests of terrorist cells in Delhi, Rajasthan and Gujarat, earning them death threats from the Indian Mujahideen.[11] Their investigations into the Malegaon blasts had provoked similar threats from Hindutva fundamentalists. In a way, the measure of honesty was simple: if both sides of the political and criminal spectrum hated you, you were probably doing something right.

Both sets of threats explained the heightened security around us. News channels breathlessly covered the allegations made in court by the Malegaon accused. According to one ATS official, these claims were 'baseless', the kind of thing that could 'hurt the sentiments of a Hindu fundamentalist.' Since the statements were made from a pay phone outside a bar, he added, the individual was most likely 'under the influence of alcohol'.[12]

The controversy intensified when it emerged that the eleven suspects arrested in the Malegaon case had links to Abhinav Bharat, a Hindutva organization. Amongst them were a former army officer, Lt Col. Shrikant Prasad Purohit, and a Hindu sadhvi, Pragya Singh Thakur.

I pieced all of it in bits and pieces over the years. In 2008, when I glanced at the paper, everything seemed twisted into simplistic narratives, of heroes and villains, of revenge on Pakistan, of whether Kasab and his group of terrorists had taken drugs, eaten cashews, or sought blessings from their mothers.

Finance, cricket and money had quickly entangled themselves with 26/11. The attacks, estimated to have cost around fifty thousand crore rupees, were not expected to have a lasting impact on the Indian stock market, reported a financial daily—terrorist attacks, after all, had become a grim routine in both India

---

[11]Mohan, Vishwa/*TNN*, 'Indian Mujahideen had warned Karkare, ATS in emails', *timesofindia.indiatimes.com*, 20 December 2008, https://tinyurl.com/3vtv695j. Accessed on 16 December 2024.

[12]Shrivastav, Vikas, 'ATS top boss gets threat call', *mumbaimirror.indiatimes.com*, 26 November 2008, https://tinyurl.com/hhyaac6k. Accessed on 16 December 2024.

and Mumbai. In a show of solidarity, the English cricket team returned for the Test series, and Sachin Tendulkar, after scoring an unbeaten century in India's victory, dedicated his innings to the victims of 26/11. Meanwhile, Maharashtra's Chief Minister, Vilasrao Deshmukh, was spotted touring the Taj Hotel with his son, actor Riteish Deshmukh, and filmmaker Ram Gopal Varma, who would later direct the widely panned *The Attacks of 26/11*.

This last act was seen as deeply insensitive and triggered a wave of resignations. Around the same time, Deputy Chief Minister R.R. Patil dismissed the attacks in an interview as a 'small incident' that happens in 'big cities', a reworking of the famous line Shah Rukh Khan's Raj tells Kajol's Simran in *Dilwale Dulhania Le Jayenge*. The backlash forced him to resign. Shivraj Patil, Union Home Minister, also stepped down amidst mounting criticism over intelligence failures, chronic underfunding of the Mumbai Police, and their lack of equipment and training.

Details soon emerged about how the Intelligence Bureau had failed to adequately warn the Mumbai Police. Reports suggested that, for over a year, intelligence officials had been aware that Mumbai was vulnerable to an attack from the sea. Even the United States had warned India before the attack

My father had even proposed increasing 'sea patrols', but his plan was buried in bureaucratic red tape. The dinghy that Ajmal Kasab and the other terrorists arrived in had, in fact, been stopped by the Navy, only to be let off after they produced false ID cards.

In the final weeks of December, almost a month after the attack, Minority Affairs Minister A.R. Antulay set off a political firestorm by suggesting that my father had been killed because of his investigation into the Malegaon blasts.

'Karkare was a very bold officer. He had vision and was prepared to lay down his life for the country. Now, how come, instead of going to the Taj or the Oberoi, he went to such a place where there was nothing?'

A view echoed by some residents of Malegaon, who had, for once, been treated fairly by India's police, an institution that had often been hostile to the Muslim community. One of them said, *'Karkare ji ko maara gaya hai kyunki sab khulaasa kar rahe the, aur kya? Ek umeed ki kiran thi hum logon ke liye, woh bhi chali gayi.' (Karkareji was killed because his investigation was going to reveal the truth. We have lost the one ray of hope we had.)*

The backlash was immediate. The BJP and Shiv Sena condemned his remarks. The Congress distanced itself, calling them his 'personal views'. Antulay later backtracked, claiming he wasn't questioning who had killed Karkare, only who had sent him in that direction.

Amidst all this chaos, it had seemed to me in 2008 as though there would never be a way to uncover what really happened. Noise, hearsay and political back and forth would drown out all the things that really mattered. I would have to wait for a day when controversy would die down, and someone would be brave and trustworthy enough to report the truth. In August 2021, investigative journalist Josy Joseph published *The Silent Coup*. I purchased the book because I had been a fan of his previous work, 2016's *A Feast of Vultures*, and found that there were several pages devoted to Pappa and his work in the ATS which focused on the Malegaon case in greater detail. I read those pages almost through the corner of my eye, still not fully ready to stare into the sun of all that had transpired in 2008.

I discovered that my father had gone to Malegaon a day after the blasts.[13] He examined the remains of a destroyed LML Freedom motorcycle, strapped with explosives, and began the investigation. The ATS identified the engine number, traced it back to an agency that sold the bike, and discovered the buyer's name: Pragya Singh Thakur, a former member of the Akhil Bhartiya Vidyarthi Parishad (ABVP), the student wing of the BJP.

---

[13]Joseph, Josy, *The Silent Coup: A History of India's Deep State* (Kindle ed.), Context, Westland Publications, New Delhi, 2021, pp. 87–88.

Soon after, under Pappa's leadership, the ATS uncovered the existence of a shadowy Hindutva terror group that included Lt Col. Prasad Shrikant Purohit, retired Major Ramesh Upadhyay, and others. The investigation revealed that the group intended to retaliate against Islamic terrorism by targeting Muslim localities.

When I went back to the *Mumbai Mirror* archives to see what Pappa had said, unable to rely on my right-wing relatives with their pro-BJP sentiments, I discovered that he had been deeply upset that his investigation was being overshadowed by religious narratives.

'I never coined that term,' my father told *Mumbai Mirror* in an interview conducted on November 26 when asked about 'Hindutva terror'.[14] 'And people who know me would know I never discriminate amongst people.'

Media commentators then and now had used labels like 'Hindutva terror' and 'Saffron terror', often linking terrorism to religion because it's easy to do so rather than question failures of intelligence, governance and security. The nature of his killing did not change what had been lost. It did not bring back Pappa, nor did it resolve the unresolved threads of our lives. Unless I somehow became all-knowing and all-powerful, which was only possible through political office, it was futile to go down such routes. The truth, it seemed, was an impossibly expensive commodity. In 2008, all I could try to do was move on.

~

I returned to my coaching classes for 12th standard and the CPT entrance for the CA exams, trying to escape the drama unfolding not only inside our house but across the country. Each teacher called me forward, assuring me they would do everything they could, because I was a martyr's son. I nodded along. My friends

---

[14]Sathe, Abhijit, 'ATS chief Karkare stood for the common man', *mumbaimirror.indiatimes.com*, 28 November 2008, https://tinyurl.com/ysntkur7. Accessed on 16 December 2024.

were awkward around me and didn't know what to say. I tried to act as normal as possible as if nothing out of the ordinary had transpired at all

Some began advising me, perhaps repeating what their parents might have said, that I was 'my mother's only hope now.' Almost everyone had a lot of advice for me, but since it always came from people who hadn't lived through what I had, I never paid it much attention. I felt as if I had aged out of my generation. My peers were concerned with board exams and school crushes; I had no words for what was going through my head, and I doubted they would understand. I suddenly found myself inside a a bubble, far apart from anyone around me. Whenever I looked at my classmates, I felt only their pitying eyes staring back at me. I didn't want that to be the story imposed on my life.

Bodyguards had started accompanying me to and from these various coaching classes, a constant reminder of everything that had happened. I wanted them gone. My friends made fun of me for having bodyguards. I found it cruel. But I suppose we were all kids then.

The truth was that the bodyguards had been around for a while without me knowing. I hadn't even realized I was being followed. Occasionally, I would notice men watching me from a distance. Once, while sitting with a friend, a man approached the watchman to ask about me.

'Did you go to a cybercafe to play video games?' Pappa had asked me once.

'What? No,' I said.

'I know you did.'

'How?'

'Terrorists go there. My people are looking into cyber cafés across Mumbai.'

Months later, the mystery solved itself.

My uncle Kiran and I had gone to an awards ceremony to receive an honour on my father's behalf. Mummy had guilt-tripped me into going. I hid from journalists, avoided their questions, stared at my feet, trying to make myself invisible. Afterward, as was our ritual, Kiran Mama and I went to Shree Datta Boarding in Parel for Malvani seafood thali. One of the men in uniform who joined us, someone my uncle knew, turned to me and said, 'I used to be your bodyguard.'

I blinked. 'What?'

'Yes.' He laughed. 'You walked so much and so fast that I had to get a bike.'

Later I told Mummy, 'I didn't know I had a bodyguard.'

'Yeah, you did.'

'What if I was hanging out with a girlfriend or smoking?' I joked.

'Their training tells them not to interfere with those things,' she said, laughing.

On the day of my first prelim exam, as I walked through the corridors, I felt everyone's eyes on me. Strangers came up to shake my hand, as if I had suddenly become Harry Potter. 'Why are you even coming for the prelims?' someone asked.

Normally I'd take any excuse to skip school.

'What else is there to do?' I replied. 'I can't stand it at home.'

That was the end of the conversation.

Then a peon approached me.

'Are you Aakash Hemant Karkare?'

I nodded.

He led me to the Vice Principal's office. She offered her condolences.

I nodded again, about to leave, when she said, 'My father died when I was young too. I was five. I barely remember him.' She laughed.

I appreciated her casual treatment of death.

'By the way, did the President visit your house?' she asked.

'I think so. I wasn't home.'

Another person looking for gossip, I thought to myself.

'So many cars these people bring. There was so much traffic on Tilak Bridge. It was so annoying.'

'Yes,' I agreed. 'It is really annoying.'

Meanwhile, A.R. Antulay's allegations had forced my mother to speak out. She said the expected things, that she was proud of her husband's sacrifice, but admitted, 'We have paid a hard price for it. It is very painful because I am fifty-plus and at this age, I really needed my husband.'

The interview was conducted in our living room. My sisters had returned to their lives in Boston and Leipzig. I wanted to return to mine in Mumbai, but the media intrusion never let up. My mother sat on the sofa, framed by a photograph of my father in the background. Everything felt staged. Our family was no longer just a family; we were slowly being turned into a symbol. A human face for the 26/11 tragedy.

I learned things I had never known before. That Pappa's 'mother was from the BJP and his father had communist ideologies, but they never argued. So he had a mix of both—that's why he investigated the Malegaon blast. For any other officer, it would have been different.'

She also mentioned that S, then twenty-three, believed Mohammed Ajmal Kasab, the lone surviving terrorist, should be given a chance 'to understand the gravity of his actions'.

The response was predictable. *Saamna* ran an outraged editorial. There was no room for nuance, no space for anything but bloodlust. Grief, in their eyes, had to be turned into anger, into demands for execution. Anything less was unacceptable.

My mother admitted she 'strongly regretted' Pappa's decision to take up the ATS post.

'When he took that job, I knew from his nature and uprightness that he would go in front and fight. It's a risky post. I used to tell him to apply for a UN job.'

She insisted he had never been under external pressure while investigating the Malegaon blasts. 'He was not confused; his ideas, his ideology were fixed. The investigation had gone smoothly, and he had finished his work.'

Despite the constant political attacks, she remained firm in her belief that he had done the right thing.

'He was criticized by various political parties, from every side. It was humiliating and sorrowful for us. But I know my husband was right. He had proof, so he was comfortable.'

She spoke about us too. The loss, she said, had been especially hard on her children. While my eldest sister, being married, had the support of her family, she noted that her younger daughter and seventeen-year-old son were struggling.

'The first month we were in too much grief. At night, they would cry, get angry, and I allowed them to show their emotions so that they could calm down.'

When I first read those words, I felt a sharp, unexpected anger. For, until then, we had barely spoken about Pappa's death. Not really.

'Why did you lie to the newspapers?' I remember yelling at Mummy. 'We haven't spoken about Pappa in the entire month since he died.'

She only stared at me, refusing to answer. Except during these angry outbursts, we hardly ever spoke about him or what had happened. I only discovered her statements later, either by googling or while researching for this memoir.

The media had by then reported every tiny detail about the attack, sometimes getting things wrong in their race for exclusives. They had even been accused of potentially aiding the terrorists, whose handlers were watching coverage to track police movements.

Each newspaper article, each comment by a politician, began to feel like an act of violence. And by giving interviews, I thought, my mother was contributing to it. I no longer wanted to hear anyone else's version of Pappa. It felt unreal, false, in conflict with my own memories.

Once, a print journalist from a magazine came over to interview my mother for a light-hearted feature. Afterwards, she knocked on my door and asked if S and I would pose for a photograph. The idea of juxtaposing a terror attack with a staged family portrait seemed grotesque to me, so I refused. She persisted. When I finally got irritated, she backed off with a breezy 'no hard feelings'.

'Why can't you protect us from these people?' I snapped later. 'You know I don't want to speak to them! They took photographs of me half-naked at Pappa's funeral! There are pictures of his dead body on the internet!' I snapped.

By then, my cynicism had hardened.

The Mumbai Police had sent blood samples of my father, along with those of officers Kamte and Salaskar, to a forensic laboratory to test for alcohol content, something experts noted was unusual in the case of a terror attack.[15]

'The police officials keep coming home and harassing me about blood tests,' Mummy complained to me.

'Let's shut the door in their face and yell at them. Let's sue them,' I'd say, bristling with anger.

'We can't do that,' she'd respond.

Like most people in India, I'd never really had any hope or faith in political figures. But in the aftermath of the 26/11 attacks, their posturing seemed that much more egregious, because it was personal.

'A party that condemns policemen one day for investigating terror suspects and then commends them the next day for dying while fighting the good fight against terror (because it sees Hindus as intrinsically innocent and Muslims as congenitally guilty) is unfit to rule,' wrote the noted author Mukul Kesavan in

[15]*PTI*, 'Blood samples of Karkare, Salaskar Amte sent for test', *timesofindia.indiatimes.com*, 23 December 2008, https://tinyurl.com/3eft5tr8. Accessed on 16 December 2024.

a *Hindustan Times* article titled 'How politicians turned this man from hero to villain to hero again'.[16] 'To defeat terrorism India needs intelligence that's gathered and acted upon by clear-eyed, even-handed policemen. The last thing we need is to have these policemen bullied by politicians who are blinkered by prejudice and made stupid by bigotry.'

'The heroic death of Maharashtra's Anti-Terrorism Squad (ATS) chief Hemant Karkare in counter-terror operations has left the BJP-Shiv Sena combine with egg on its face,' went an article in *The Economic Times*. 'On Friday, Narendra Modi, BJP's poster-boy chief minister and Hindutva mascot, paid lofty tributes to Karkare and other senior cops who lost their lives in the counter attack. But before his death on duty, Mr Karkare and his colleagues at the ATS were at the receiving end of almost a slanderous attack not only by BJP and Shiv Sena leaders, but also by several Sangh Parivar organizations for the ongoing ATS probe into the Malegaon blasts. But the two parties are now singing eulogies to the valour demonstrated by the departed ATS chief.'[17]

Shiv Sena had even planned a band on 1 December to protest the arrests of the accused, Pragya Singh Thakur and Lt Col. Purohit.

So, by 26 January 2009, when I accompanied Mummy to Delhi to receive the Ashoka Chakra on my father's behalf, I had already lost complete faith in journalists, politicians and the government. Reading George Orwell's novels on politics *1984* and *Animal Farm* at fifteen, both part of Pappa's personal library, had only sharpened that disillusionment. I went to Delhi only because my mother complained about having to fulfil these

---

[16]Kesavan, Mukul, 'How politicians turned this man from hero to villain to hero again', *hindustantimes.com*, 29 November 2008, https://tinyurl.com/5xh5w3xn. Accessed on 16 December 2024.

[17]ET Bureau, 'Parivar doublespeak: Villain in life, hero in death', *economictimes.indiatimes.com*, 29 November 2008, https://tinyurl.com/mrp9eaxk. Accessed on 16 December 2024.

government obligations on her own.

My mother, a *kaka*, and I travelled to Delhi for the ceremony. Almost instantly I regretted coming. The entire spectacle felt hollow. The crowds, the uniforms, the performance of the state.

'Didn't your father rush into battle?' Someone at the hotel asked me. I was too shy to answer. 'No, that's not true,' I mumbled.

Later, I realized this was the government's preferred narrative. A way to shift blame from the systems that had failed.

That evening, we were invited to Rashtrapati Bhavan for dinner with the president. My mother thought this might be a good chance to speak. Instead, we stood in a line, and the president passed by, waved, before disappearing into another chamber. A photo-op. The government was eager to claim someone they could use as a symbol.

One December morning, Kiran Mama and I drove to Girgaum Chowpatty in his hatchback. A few relatives came along. On my lap, in the passenger seat, rested a clay pot filled with fragments of bone and a handful of brown ash. In the backseat sat the *sahitya* for the ritual, yellow flowers, white thread, incense, and a coconut, as always.

Years earlier, Pappa had driven S, J and me to this very spot when we lived in a government quarters on Nepean Sea Road. I must have been seven or eight. We had come for *visarjan*, carrying the small Ganpati idol we kept at home. The only time we had done something like that. I remember Pappa paying a man on the beach to swim into the sea, immerse the idol, and return with a small mound of wet mud where it had been placed.

We parked near the restaurant called Ideal Café and crossed the road to the beach. As we walked across the sand, I recalled a grim joke I'd overheard a few days earlier:

'They just reach into the furnace and pull out whatever's left.

Who knows whose ashes we're actually holding?'

I placed the pot and other materials on the surface of the Arabian Sea. The pot upturned, and bits of bone and ash floated briefly before the waves drew them away. The 8 a.m. sun was just beginning to scald my skin. On either side of me, various kakas and mamas stood with folded hands and shut eyes. A policeman, perhaps a beach guard, watched silently. I wondered if what we were doing technically counted as littering.

The rituals stretched on, long after any physical trace of Pappa had dissolved into the sea. There was something on the fifth day. Then the seventh. Then the tenth. Each ceremony involved ponderous, half-naked priests droning in Sanskrit inside hot, stuffy rooms thick with fire, smoke, and the smell of camphor.

But for Pappa, and because Mummy believed in it, just this one time and never again, I told myself.

An *atya*, paternal aunt, had explained that these ceremonies were necessary for the great-grandfather to attain *moksha*, liberation. In some kind of purgatory, three generations of my ancestors sat waiting for their next of kin to die, so a male offspring could light the pyre and complete the cycle. Now, Pappa had joined Ajoba, who would finally get moksha when my own pyre was lit by my son. It all sounded like something out of a fantasy novel.

One ritual, *Kaksparsh*, involved leaving food out for the crows. The faster they touched it, the more the dead person's wishes were believed to be fulfilled. Pappa's plate was touched at once.

'Because he died a martyr's death, on the battlefield,' a relative said. 'All his dreams were fulfilled.'

How could a fifty-four-year-old man, still six years from retirement, with so many lives left to lead, have fulfilled all his wishes?

If nothing else, the rituals gave me something to focus on, something other than the many afterlives of 26/11, which by then had splintered into several threads.

My mother would criticize the government, or a politician would make a controversial comment. R.R. Patil once claimed that my father had come to him with tears in his eyes on the night of his death.[18]

> 'On November 26, Karkare came with the entire ATS team to meet me at around 2030 hrs. He was with me till 2130 hrs. With tears rolling down his eyes, Karkare told me about the allegations being levelled against him (in Malegaon blasts case),' Patil said. 'Soon after Karkare left, came the news of his being killed. Maybe that was destiny,' Patil said.

Then Mummy would be hounded for days to respond. Media professionals who pretended to be her friends pressured her to speak. One by one, they would trickle in, fishing for a new statement. And then, a few days later, they would return, seeking her response to the politician's response to her response.

So, at seventeen, I'd stopped believing in most things. Family. Government. Politicians. A terrible cocktail.

---

[18]*PTI*, 'Karkare wept over Malegaon charges, says R R Patil', *rediff.com*, 16 December 2008, https://tinyurl.com/r2jy56a5. Accessed on 16 December 2024.

6

Walking away

I knew I had to leave Mumbai the day I became trapped in the get-together room, unable to go to the bathroom.

The entire living room was jam-packed with TV reporters, cameras and print journalists. My mother sat in the middle of our light-brown sofa, answering questions. The only way to the toilet was through this crowd. I tried to gesture to someone in the kitchen that I needed the back door opened, but Lata Bai didn't notice.

So I sat in bed, staring at the ceiling, waiting for the journalists to leave.

At first, I laughed at the absurdity of it—like something out of the 1990s US sitcom *Seinfeld*. But then I thought: *If I stayed here, in this house, in this city, surrounded by these reminders, I would never be able to put any distance between 26/11 and myself. I would never be able to move on. Somehow, I needed to escape.*

During the remaining months of 12th standard, I tried to escape the shadow of what had happened, never mentioning it to friends or discussing it with anyone. If the topic arose, I grew awkward. I had always been shy. I tried to ignore the way 26/11 lingered in our lives by shutting myself inside my room. Once, my best friend said, 'If I were in your place, I wouldn't have just stayed shut inside my room.'

The words made my skin burn. *If I were in your place.* As if he could imagine it. As if he could understand. But I said nothing. I still didn't know how to put my feelings about my father into words. I wasn't even sure what I felt.

Another friend asked about a CNG that Murli Deora, the petroleum minister, had given my mother. Yet another about the flat we had gotten. I only ever heard about these things as gossip about my own life. It made me want to break off all ties with anyone who knew these things about me. It seemed like no one had any sensitivity. Only vulgar curiosity.

I kept telling my mother not to accept these things. To give them back. To refuse. After all, it was the government that had failed us.

'People want to help. We should let them,' she replied.

A gap began to form between us.

I spent most of my time holed up in my bedroom. I emerged only at night, poking through the fridge for leftovers or wandering aimlessly through the streets of Dadar TT and Matunga. Was it grief? I couldn't say. I didn't feel anything at all.

Bombay Aaji had moved in to keep Mummy company. Sometimes we'd sit and talk about the TV shows she watched. That was the extent of my socialization. Since we never really ate meals together as a family, my mother and I hardly spent any time together.

Mummy spent most of her time either at college or surrounded by a sea of relatives. They sat solemnly, staring at my mother, saying the same hollow things—how sorry they were, how shocking it all was, how we should call if we ever need anything. Mummy sometimes itched to return to her old life, her college, her swimming, but with relatives constantly dropping by to judge, she held back. She'd sometimes lie to them that she was unwell so she could go for a swim.

'What's the big deal?' I asked. 'Just go for a swim. Forget them.'

'No, what will society think?' she replied.

'Who cares?'

'You don't understand now. You'll know when you are older.'

It was just another reason I resented my extended

Maharashtrian family. Their world was a web of empty performances. Upholding its principles meant you could never truly live, never choose happiness for yourself. For most of my life, 'Marathi' and 'Maharashtrian' had been symbols of the bad and boring. Now, more than ever, I felt like my childhood instincts had been right.

The house had become a shrine to Pappa. Both living rooms were filled with memorabilia—plaques, medals, framed photographs. In one, he was in a navy-blue suit, accepting a medal from the former prime minister Atal Bihari Vajpayee. In another, he was impossibly young, full head of hair, no pink bags under his eyes, standing at the IPS training centre in Hyderabad. I avoided these rooms as much as I could. It was where Mummy was forced to perform her grief for the cameras.

The guards remained stationed outside European Quarters. A paranoid *mami*, maternal aunt, had convinced Mummy that, just like the Kandahar hijacking, she could be taken hostage by the Lashkar-e-Taiba to secure Kasab's release. I argued against it, insisting Mummy send the guards back so that life could be normal again. So that the policemen could go back to doing their actual jobs. But she refused. In her vulnerable state, she clung to their warnings, as if paranoia itself could shield her from the unthinkable happening again.

I still saw my friends sometimes, after coaching classes, on the rare evening out, but something had shifted. Most of our friendship, like most at seventeen, was built on teasing, inside jokes, effortless laughter. Now I felt like I was hiding an entire side of myself. I couldn't talk to them about my complicated feelings. Even if I tried, what would they understand? They were seventeen. I felt older. Conversations about CAs, crushes, and college plans felt distant, like distant voices from a life I had once inhabited but no longer belonged to.

Pappa's death had taken with it an entire way of thinking, being and feeling. There was no opposing force in my life anymore. But acknowledging that I was suffering felt like an act of cowardice.

The computer had become my favourite companion then.

In 11th standard, after a long scolding from Pappa for forgetting to switch off the PC at noon, when downloads were charged per MB, while trying to get *The Lord of the Rings* trilogy, I scoured the neighbourhood for a better solution and found a local internet connection called Five Net. With unlimited access, my days at coaching classes dwindled. Instead, I stayed locked in my room, hosting private film festivals. I started with the comedies of Kevin Smith and Judd Apatow, reassuring myself that since I could laugh at movies again, I must have healed.

S tried talking to me about Pappa once, but I brushed it off. What was there to say? He was dead. There was nothing we could do. If I ever felt bad, I comforted myself with metaphysical theories: people never really died; they came back whenever we thought of them. Or maybe it was string theory: Pappa was only gone in this universe, but alive somewhere else. Either way, there was no point dwelling on it.

I kept going deeper into film, through the French New Wave of Godard and Truffaut, the European classics of Fellini and Bergman, the nineties American indie cinema of Linklater, and the documentaries of Herzog. I was particularly drawn to films about fractured families, father-son relationships, and the struggle to connect with parents, or what to do in their absence. I gravitated toward stories about government apathy and the tangled web of global politics, like the satirical film about the Bosnian war, *No Man's Land* (2001), and the animated anti-war film *Waltz with Bashir*.

The ending of *No Man's Land*, where the UN lies to journalists while one of the protagonists remains stranded on an undiffused mine, felt particularly cathartic.

In Frederico Fellini's *La Dolce Vita* (1960), there's a scene where Marcello Mastroianni's paparazzo colleague ruthlessly exploits a grieving family after the father's suicide. The moment filled me with such rage that I had to switch off the film. In *Ikiru* (1954), Akira Kurosawa depicts a once-scorned bureaucrat being celebrated on his death anniversary by the very colleagues who had spent years despising him. At the end of *Mumbai Meri Jaan* (2007), Soha Ali Khan's character, who is a journalist, struggles to talk about her dead husband and keeps breaking into tears.

When I look back on that seventeen-year-old version of myself, beyond the anger, there's an overwhelming feeling of numbness. Life occurred around me. I wasn't always sad. I wasn't always happy. Mostly, I was calm, observing my life with an air of detachment. I was aloof, lost in my dream world, and kept retreating further into it. Things like the HSC exams and CA seemed almost pointless in the wake of what had happened. Not in a grandiose way, but simply because if death could so abruptly put a full stop to our lives, shouldn't I be giving more thought to how I was living mine? Shouldn't life feel more important, more urgent, if we are going to die anyway?

For the first time, I became aware of my own mortality.

I had picked commerce without much thought. Mummy had always insisted I study whatever made the most money, carried the best designation, and ensured good standing in society, so she could boast to her relatives. That was fine by me. I wanted as much money as possible, too, enough to escape my parents' influence, live on my own, and eventually become a writer at forty.

In school, I assumed the best way to do this was IIT. Every week, *Education Times* ran headlines about students landing eighty- to ninety-crore placements after doing an IIT and IIM. That would be more than enough, I thought. But during the summer after 10th, I discovered, to my horror, that IIT coaching classes began on 13 April, barely two weeks after school ended. Since I knew I'd do an MBA anyway, I figured commerce was the easier path. IIT wasn't worth sacrificing the five months of summer vacations between 10th and 11th standard—the break I had been looking forward to all through school. Like most commerce students, I enrolled in CPT coaching, the first step towards becoming a CA.

What I really wanted to study, though, was humanities. I wanted to be a writer. But that meant no money, and worse, endless arguments. Both Mummy and Pappa believed humanities were for the soft-hearted and for women. I didn't agree, but I had no interest in another long-drawn-out battle. So I postponed the decision until after I took my 12th board exams. Based on how well I did, I thought I'd know what to choose. I never really liked studying. I was a dreamer, spending most of my time on the back benches, gazing out of the window. One of my happiest memories was when my teacher sent me home with a bad remark in my calendar: '*Dreaming in class.*'

Even so I found it quite easy to get decent-ish marks without much effort, marks that were never enough for my parents. When I told Pappa I'd scored 83% in 10th, the first thing he said was: 'My office boy's son got 90% without him having to pay 40,000 rupees for his coaching classes.'

I had barely studied all year, cramming only through sleepless nights before exams. Most of them went fine. I even registered for the Common Law Admission Test because I'd heard the National Law School in Bangalore was called the 'Harvard of the East.' Getting an education there felt like a great adventure.

That summer, while waiting for my results, I immersed myself in *Six Feet Under*, the HBO drama about a family that runs a funeral home. In the first episode, the patriarch, Nate Fisher, dies suddenly like Pappa, but in a car accident. He reappears as a recurring figure for his children, guiding them through grief. Each episode opened with a death, making mortality feel like an ordinary fact of life. In one flashback, Claire, the youngest Fisher child, seventeen, like I was then, tells her father she's afraid of death. 'There's nothing to fear,' he replies, urging her to touch the body he's preparing. She describes it as a wall: cool to touch, not scary at all.

But the show didn't portray death as simple. The Fishers screamed, fought, exploded. They had the option of privacy, no TV cameras or political statements, and certainly not the hundred thousand relatives Indians seemed to have.

'You can pump him full of chemicals,' one brother yells. 'You can put makeup on him. You can prop him up in the slumber room. But the fact remains, David, the only father we're ever gonna have is gone. Forever. And that sucks. But it's life. You can't accept it without getting your hands dirty.'

David, the stoic son, eventually breaks when he sees the bus that killed his father.

Pappa's death wasn't like that. There was no bus, no visible culprit. Instead, there was a courtroom and a trial. Intelligence failures. Media narratives that shifted every week. Global politics, geopolitics, terror. Gossip and hearsay. Ever-changing facts.

Six Feet Under made me face the aspects of death I couldn't think about—bodies, blood, the betrayals of biology, the inevitability of ageing—subjects society leaves no room for, because no one really wants to dwell on them.

The only National Law College I got into was the one in Raipur, a new campus without rankings. The *Outlook* list said the fourth best law college was ILS Pune. I'd never heard of it, but looking at past admissions, I saw that as long as you had 70% in 12th, you got in. That felt like a low bar for the fourth best college in India, and I was sure I'd clear it.

These decisions happened entirely outside Mummy's orbit. I made them alone, in secret, between my little film festivals at home. One day, my friends and I planned to submit our CPT forms at the CA Institute in Cuffe Parade before hanging out at Marine Drive and walk around South Mumbai before coming home.

'Where are all of you headed?' Mummy asked them as I was tying my shoelaces.

'We're going to pay our CPT fees,' one of them told her.

'Aakash, why haven't you taken any money to fill these forms?' Mummy asked me.

'Because I am not appearing for the CA entrance,' I replied. 'I am doing law.'

Before she could react, I walked out of the front door and my friends joined me. We didn't talk about my deception. Mummy kept calling; I ignored her until I couldn't. When I finally picked up, she was enraged.

'Well, if you didn't know I was not going for CPT classes until now, then you obviously don't care.'

She didn't respond after that and hung up.

Over the next few days, she frantically called relatives to try and convince me not to do law. One by one, they came home and tried to convince me that I was too innocent for such a corrupt world. That without a father or grandfather as a lawyer, I couldn't survive. These were the same relatives who plastered Pappa's face on their phone wallpapers, name-dropped him for small favours, spoke of revenge on Pakistan, supported the RSS and the BJP, and at the same time, sang paeans to him.

Then someone told Mummy about corporate law placements and ILS's 'dedicated' teachers. If I went there, they said, my life would change for the better. Eventually, she came around. She wasn't thrilled about Pune, but by then, I felt she had begun living her own life anyway. My anger at her made leaving easier. It dulled the guilt. She had her relatives and friends. She would be fine. Besides she had two more children, and both had left, so why did I have to stay? And I would finally be free. To find something, anything, beyond the suffocating atmosphere at home.

I scored 78% in the HSC board exams. Soon after, Mummy and the elderly melodramatic relative insisted I give interviews.

'Why?' I'd asked.

'They want you to give a message of hope.'

'What would that do?' I'd asked again.

'To inspire the youth of India.'

'To do what? Give 12th standard exams? Don't most of the youth of India already do that?'

We all laughed.

'Karkare's son comes out in flying colours in HSC exams,'[19] reported an *NDTV* headline, adding: *'17-year-old Akash had appeared for the HSC exams even though he was in a state of trauma due to the death of his father.'*

Another headline in *Mid-Day* ran: *'His father's death did not deter him.' Adding that, 'he determinedly appeared for his HSC board exams earlier this year.'*[20]

'Nobody forced him or encouraged him to appear. He convinced himself to take the exams,' my mother was quoted as saying in the article.

Was this true? I couldn't tell anymore. Was I suffering from trauma? Was I brave for appearing for board exams? Not appearing for them had never been an option. Such a thing had never appeared in my mind. Losing a year was a scandal in the extended Karkare family. My mother spoke in whispers about faraway relatives who had failed in their exams. Or scored less than eighty in 10th or 12th standard.

It wasn't as if I had gone to war. I had simply sat for the same exam hundreds of thousands of others did. Plenty must have gone through worse. Life goes on. The past had to be left behind.

But journalists needed narratives. They needed characters to slot into roles. We became one: the martyr's family. A type easier to write about than to live.

Some reporters showed up a few days after the results came in. My mother, too polite to refuse, let them in. I found myself sitting in the living room across from a journalist who insisted a

---

[19]*PTI*, 'Karkare's son comes out in flying colours in HSC exams', *ndtv.com*, 4 June 2009, https://tinyurl.com/ycyzp7hd. Accessed on 16 December 2024.

[20]Vibhute, Kranti, 'His father's death did not deter him', *mid-day.com*, 4 June 2009, https://tinyurl.com/4bp5m8m8. Accessed on 16 December 2024.

framed photo of my father be in the background. I felt a mix of irritation and resignation.

'Did your father give you any advice before he passed?' they asked.

I hesitated for a moment. Then lied. 'Live your life without caring what people say about you. They will keep talking. Do things because you want to.'

Pappa wasn't one really to sit down and give you advice. But was anyone really? Didn't those kinds of portrayals mostly exist in sitcoms and cheesy movies?

Later, Mummy asked when he had told me that. I admitted I made it up. She said I should have thought of something better because it sounded rude.

'Well,' I said. 'What was I supposed to say? The last piece of advice he gave me was that once you get fat cells, they stay with you forever? And that I needed to be careful because I was getting a lot of fat cells around my stomach?'

It was genuinely the last piece of advice or feedback I remember him giving me. Journalists wanted grand lines; all I had were bitter fragments.

I applied to just one college, refusing to use RA Podar as a backup for a BCom degree. I got admission to ILS in the fourth merit list. I packed my father's old hard-case suitcase with clothes, slipped the family laptop into a backpack, and added a few books and my tennis racket.

When a borrowed car arrived, I got in with my mother and a kaka who wanted a ride. I played *Breathe Me* by Sia, the same song Claire Fisher had chosen for her drive to New York, leaving everything behind to become a photographer. While my mother and uncle made idle conversation, a strange electricity coursed through me. I wasn't sure if I was excited or afraid. Probably both. But as we climbed the ghats of the Western Express Highway, the weight of the past loosened its grip.

Part II

Anywhere But Home

(2009–13)

'What the deuce is it to me?' He interrupted impatiently;
'you say that we go round the sun.
If we went round the moon it would not make
a pennyworth of difference to me or to my work.'

—Sherlock Holmes in *A Study in Scarlet*, Arthur Conan Doyle

1

The fourth best law college in India

I went to college not believing in much about the world. I felt misunderstood by everyone around me, weighed down by some kind of external pressure I couldn't name. My idols were the brothers from the Japanese anime *Full Metal Alchemist,* who burnt their homes so they wouldn't have a place to return to. That's what I wanted too, to keep moving forward, to watch my past recede into the distance. Maybe I was depressed, but I didn't know it then.

In law school, touted as the fourth best in the country, I hoped to find answers to all the questions that haunted me. I imagined I'd meet friends who understood me, people I could finally reveal my hidden self to. I was tired of people mistaking my shyness for innocence, or worse, stupidity. I always had many things to say but always doubted anyone would understand, doubly so after the preceding year. College, I told myself, would change that.

I had heard that the teachers at ILS were incredibly dedicated to their students, that the reputations of the National Law Schools were overblown, and that the 'real truth' about the law was to be found in this university. I had always dreamt of an education like that, where teachers spoke to your soul, where they opened doors to ideas and worlds you didn't even know existed.

I had grown up in Mumbai, in a lousy school with indifferent teachers. Education had never really spoken to me. I could never pay attention to any of the lectures in school; to me, real life existed somewhere outside the confines of the classroom walls. On the streets, with friends, playing cricket or climbing trees.

Inside the hot, stifling classroom, my mind drifted elsewhere. My gaze would go slack, my thoughts wandering to faraway lands. Some pop-culture-savvy classmates started calling me 'the deadman' or 'the zombie'.

At first, I hated that my mind worked this way. After too much teasing, I resolved to stop daydreaming in class. I even came up with an equation to stop the habit: there were only so many thoughts in a day. The problem was I wasn't doing enough thinking at home, so I arrived at school with a surplus. If I thought hard enough in the evenings, rather than watching TV, I would 'use up' my quota and be free to concentrate in class. Needless to say, it didn't work. The moment a teacher started speaking, I drifted off.

Eventually, I stopped fighting my natural state of being and accepted the situation.

In college, I wanted this to change. It was there where all the great thinkers of the world had been created. I pictured myself like Alexander, learning from Aristotle, fully engaged in ideas, my mind no longer restless but focused. For once, I wanted all my faculties to be alive in the classroom, as they had been on a tennis court years earlier. Where I wouldn't be bored and wouldn't feel like my entire life was passing me by.

I imagined meeting teachers who sort of would become my surrogate parents, guiding me into the world of thought and ideas, helping me create a philosophy to understand the world. If I could just grasp the rules that governed society, I told myself, I might unlock the meaning of life, the universe, and everything in between. Something more profound than Douglas Adams' '42'. If only I'd known from the start that this was a doomed project.

Looking back, I see that what I expected from teachers, the institution, even my peers, was what people often expect from love. As Woody Allen put it in *Crimes and Misdemeanors*: 'When we fall in love, we are seeking to re-find all or some of the people to whom we were attached as children. On the other hand, we ask our beloved to correct all of the wrongs that these early parents or siblings inflicted upon us. So that love contains in it the contradiction: the attempt to return to the past and the attempt to undo the past.'

No teacher, let alone the fourth best law college in India, could ever live up to that standard.

On my first morning in the ILS men's hostel, I opened a bathroom door to find a pile of faeces. I spun around and ran out. 'Get used to it.' A senior laughed from the railing. 'Every year the hostel runs out of water for weeks.'

The campus itself was sprawling: a cricket ground, tennis court, swimming pool, and classrooms large enough to comfortably seat a hundred students at the kind of heavy wooden desks that always reminded me of *Kuch Kuch Hota Hai.* Lush greenery surrounded us, and a nearby middle-class hangout, simply called The Hill, was considered part of campus. That's where students went to smoke or drink Old Monk or Royal Stag. Unfortunately, I had been conditioned by a lifetime of advice from Mummy and Pappa that only 'bad boys' did such activities, so I avoided them completely.

The first two years of the five-year course didn't even include law. Instead, we studied English, Legal Language, Economics, History, and Political Science under the Bachelor of Legal Sciences program. The LL.B. subjects began in the third year. Lectures started at 7 a.m., ending by 8.30 some days, 10.30 on others.

After class, the day stretched endlessly. Some of us, like me, caught up on sleep. Many struggled with so much unstructured time for the first time in their lives. Boredom reigned. People wandered the grounds, the canteen, the cricket field, talking about football and girls. None of this interested me. I wanted to talk about books, films, life, death. In my head, I was an artist, but everyone else was in law school.

'My soul died in law school,' I wrote in a journal, one I kept hidden underneath my pillow, something I turned to whenever despair set in. Secretly, I hoped to become an artist someday, to salvage something from this wasted time. Now I find it pretentious, but also tender, that my younger self was struggling to believe in a world that felt hostile to my very being. In those pages, mixed with film reviews, story drafts, half-written novels, several narratives emerged from my undated ramblings. The primary was essentially that I was depressed.

Oh, if only I had believed myself then. At seventeen, I thought depression was just extreme sadness, not a medical condition. That happened to other people. As far as I knew, there were two camps: those who thought it was fake, a state of mind; and those who saw it as neurological. My idol Werner Herzog belonged to the first camp and I agreed. I doubted medication or therapy could help. Even if I wanted to try psychotherapy, I didn't know how. With hindsight, I see how naïve that was.

Years later, someone reading a draft of this memoir suggested I might have had PTSD after my father's death. Watching the Netflix show *Never Have I Ever* in 2020, where the protagonist is assigned a therapist after losing her father, made me wonder how differently my life might have unfolded had I spoken to someone. Instead, I buried everything—hopelessness, anger, grief. They weren't real, I told myself. They were weaknesses. Only *doing* mattered. The mind played tricks; best to ignore it.

Within months of starting law school, I realized the whole endeavour was a mistake. So did many of my peers. Escape plans flourished. Maybe the third-best law school in Delhi would be better. Maybe the number one school in Bangalore. Many even prepared to sit for the CLAT exam again. By then, I was too cynical. One year of five was done. I didn't want to make it six years of hell.

Perhaps the real problem was that I had too much time. With only four subjects per semester and two or three lectures a day, most afternoons were empty. You could cram for a week and pass the exams. Days stretched out endlessly, and all the thoughts I had long buried resurfaced.

Seneca had written about this centuries ago, that idleness and isolation could bring forth the consequences of a wrongly lived life. Consequences usually hidden by busyness. The symptoms could include dissatisfaction, self-loathing, fear, indecisiveness, lethargy and melancholy. Abandoning work, he warned, unleashes spiritual ills, especially if you fill the void by endlessly reading, or worse, collecting books to admire their spines. If only I had read Seneca then, maybe I could have avoided the path I was already stumbling down.

One could almost sense the overwhelming boredom everywhere—in the canteen, the library, the study room. Students who had spent their school years locked into ten-hour days followed by coaching classes now had nothing to do after the daily two hours of lectures. They had all believed this was the fourth best law college in the country, and now that they were here, the dream was dead. Some teachers recited entire lectures from memory, losing their place if interrupted by a question. If this was the quality of teaching at the *fourth best law college in India*, what hope was there anywhere else? 'Only those who can't do anything else, do law,' we would grimly quote to one another from Anurag Kashyap's *Gulaal*. I had wanted revelations and intellectual stimulation. This was anything but.

Most of the time in college was spent in the canteen and calculating attendance. You needed 75% to sit for exams. Between 50 and 75, you had to pay a fine of 250 rupees. Below that, you lost the year. I often felt like a character in an existential novel, like the one in Camus's *The Plague*, who notices the passage of time only by passing peas from one jug to another.

A bad education for fifteen years of my life had left my mind in a muddle, and my father's death had challenged everything I thought I knew. I wanted to unlearn all of it and create a new mind. So I searched endlessly, for meaning, for clarity, through books, movies, conversations, and experiences. But in the process, I became like someone adrift in an existential novel: detached, unable to connect with anything outside myself. Sometimes, I wondered if I had simply woken up one day like this, or if, by reading so many of those novels, I had unconsciously forced myself into the role.

Dropping out wasn't an option in my family. Instead, I fantasized about a radical change in the education system. If the point was just exams and degrees, why not compress it all into six months of exams and finish a law degree in a year instead of five? So much time saved! Life was short. I could die at any moment. Obsessed with my own mortality, I couldn't bear the thought of wasting five years in a college where nothing was taught and exams could be passed with first class by studying a single day before.

I often wondered whether my inability to make friends came from joining college late, off the fourth merit list, a month behind everyone else. Or maybe it was because I lived alone in the hostel's largest room, once occupied by former Chief Minister Vilasrao Deshmukh. Perhaps I had simply left the small pond of Mumbai, where I knew what kind of people to expect, and for the first time, was encountering students from across India. But mostly, I think I had forgotten how to socialize. I longed for deep connections but had no clue how to make them. Everyone around me was seventeen or eighteen, just like I was, yet emotionally I seemed elsewhere. Maybe I was still reeling from 26/11, but almost a year had passed. How could I still be suffering? That would be childish.

Maybe I'd spent far too much time locked inside my room.

Instead of college being the place where I opened up, the opposite happened. The fact that strangers already knew an intimate part of my life, before I could even tell them, only compounded my shyness. They had their own opinions about it, and I dreaded the moment it might come up in conversation. I feared someone I thought could be a friend would bring it up carelessly, and that friendship would be doomed. The awkward moment never failed to arrive. In every new conversation, the question lurked, unspoken but inevitable. Even the simplest 'what does your father do?' made my stomach clench, my mind racing for the least painful way to answer. 'He passed away.' 'He's no more.' 'He died last year.' I always prayed they wouldn't ask how. Thankfully, no one ever did.

I could sense those conversations approaching long before they happened. And each time, overwhelmed by discomfort, I'd retreat before they could arrive.

In the first couple of weeks, when the entire first-year batch went to a local sugarcane juice stall, the owner came straight to me: 'I know who you are. I am from Ashok Kamte's town.' I nodded and glanced around. My friends' faces were unreadable. I gulped my drink and walked away.

The morning of the fresher's party, I went to a local barber, excited for a date later. He cut my hair, then offered a facial, then a steam, and I kept saying yes. From eighty rupees, the bill swelled to five hundred. When he asked my name, I hesitated, then gave it. Immediately, he began asking about my father: which politicians had visited, how much compensation we'd received. I couldn't leave, his razor was at my neck and still some beard to go.

Despite my best efforts, seniors eventually cornered me outside the hostel gates, introducing me to a student from Malegaon who earnestly thanked me for my father's 'impartial investigation.' Their intentions were kind, but by then I had developed an almost Pavlovian response to such encounters: a tightening in my chest, a knot in my stomach. One of those seniors began seeking me out regularly, initiating friendly conversations. I kept my distance, wary of the strange hierarchies of law school. Unlike in Mumbai, juniors here were expected to call seniors *bhaiyya*. Ignoring this ritual, I was warned, could sour your entire college experience.

During a mid-term weekend at home, my mother asked if that senior was my friend. I admitted I knew him but clarified he wasn't. She explained that his father, a Congress politician, had suggested she join the party since our 'sons were such good friends.' It was the third political party to approach her. The Shiv Sena had already sent a man in orange socks, dismissing my father as 'just a government servant' and insisting my mother could achieve more as an elected official, ignoring the harassment we had endured from them. Even the Aam Aadmi Party had reached out, with Meera Sanyal making similar suggestions. Each time, my mother politely declined. She was a teacher, she said, not a politician.

Sometimes strangers would bring up details of my life I had never shared: 'Didn't you have a dog named Bruno?' 'Didn't your mother visit Beed last month?' 'I've passed your house in Dadar TT.'

And so I drifted back into my room, back to my little rituals, my laptop on my stomach, my steel bed with its thin 300-rupee mattress.

One night, a 'parasite' roommate, campus term for those who lived in the hostel without paying the fee, was staying in our room for a few weeks. Late one night, the conversation turned to parents. It was one of those nights where defences break down and the conversations turn philosophical. One friend confessed how little time he had spent with his father, and how it was now too late to make amends. Another joined in, sharing his own grief. I felt an odd relief. Not everyone had perfect parents, after all. I had been waiting for such a moment. As a child, I never spoke about my parents because I thought it too shameful to admit they argued constantly and that I never enjoyed being with them. Later, I stayed silent because Pappa had become *26/11 Martyr Hemant Karkare*.

'You're right, man,' I said. 'Fathers are a tough bunch. They can't show emotion. They don't love you.'

'Yeah,' my classmate replied, launching into another tirade about his father before eventually asking, 'What does your father do?'

Fear and awkwardness overtook me. I didn't know how to respond.

'Nothing.'

That was honest, wasn't it? Dead people don't do anything.

'Nothing? How can he do nothing?' he asked incredulously.

I fumbled for words.

'He was an IPS officer,' the other boy in the room said quietly.

Unable to bear the awkward silence any longer, I blurted, 'Have you heard of Hemant Karkare?'

Recognition flashed across his face, quickly followed by embarrassment. A heavy silence settled over the room. Soon the lights went off, and everyone went to sleep. I knew then that there would be no more revelatory conversations for me in college.

I felt lonely in a way in which I had never felt before, one that takes on a character of its own, that hung around me like a dark cloud. The moment of connection simply eluded me. It felt like I was inside a bubble, nothing I ever did would be able to pierce it and reach the world outside. I would sit at bus stops for hours on end in the evening, listening to music albums that articulated how I felt, 'The Suburbs' by Arcade Fire, or sometimes Amit Trivedi's *Dev D*. At other times, I just stared at the sky, watching the evening dissolve into night, clinging to the one thin thread of hope: that one day, I would graduate and escape this hellhole, this world of people I could not understand, who could not understand me.

So, I retreated further into pop culture, the refuge I had turned to after my father's death. I disappeared into the films of Federico Fellini, Ingmar Bergman, Akira Kurosawa, Werner Herzog, Richard Linklater. There, finally, I found the connection that had eluded me in real life. Even if no one around me understood, I could take solace in knowing that someone, somewhere, did.

I identified with the broken and the lost in independent films. Christopher McCandless in *Into the Wild* (2007) was my hero because he leaves everything behind and hitchhikes across the United States. In the Italian miniseries *The Best of Youth*, the character I most related to hurls himself out of a window mid-sentence, book still in hand. The saddest film I saw was *Nights of Cabiria*. Giulietta Masina, Fellini's Cabiria, was like a female Chaplin, her childlike face and luminous eyes unforgettable. She lingered with me long after the credits rolled. Would I too end up like her, hopeful but slowly crushed by a world that refused to make room for me?

Still, I kept trying. My idols became Camus, Kafka, Herzog, who revealed the absurdity of existence; Douglas Adams and Terry Pratchett, who mocked it with wit; Bergman and *Six Feet Under*, for daring to live alongside death; Kevin Smith, because sometimes you just needed to laugh. I obsessively read their interviews, combed through their Wikipedia pages, searching for clues on how to leave behind the world I was stuck in and join theirs, a pursuit of meaning, of what it meant to be human.

I think this kind of thinking did two things for me. First, it allowed me not to avoid confronting what I was actually feeling. I believed the real solution lay in building a life closer to my dreams, and once I had that, the depression would vanish. Second, it allowed me to believe in a better future, a world where I was happy, where life felt worthwhile. But looking back, I see the trap. While it delayed the need to face myself, it also made everything in the present feel pointless, because nothing could shake off the listlessness that had rooted itself inside me.

The happiest I was that first year was in my dusty hostel room, lying on my bed with my laptop on my stomach, lost in movies that transported me elsewhere. Briefly, I came alive again when I joined a group for a college festival play. Acting unlocked something in me. I could be my true self on stage in a way I never could one-on-one. I wasn't afraid of public speaking, but conversations always left me tongue-tied. Acting was different, I could pretend, I could say aloud the things I kept hidden. I decided then that if I ever wanted to be happy, my work would have to make me feel as alive as I did while performing.

I remember overhearing a senior asking his father for blessings before going on stage. I had no one to ask. Even when my father was alive, I wouldn't have done it. Still, I wanted something like that. So I chose to ask for blessings from Werner Herzog, alive, and resembling my father in some way.

I had imagined law school would be serious, rigorous, a place where I would finally understand the world. Instead, it felt like five more years of killing time. This couldn't be my escape. Maybe I should become a filmmaker, I thought. But the dream felt impossible.

That summer, between my first and second year, I discovered graphic novels. One book stayed with me: *Fun Home* by Alison Bechdel. In it, she dissects her relationship with her father, circling around his possible suicide with a mix of detachment and precision. The sheer honesty stunned me. Writing about one's parents without reverence or duty felt unthinkable in India. Even thinking about my father with clarity was hard, let alone writing about him. But maybe, if I could, it would help me work through my feelings. Maybe I could fictionalize it. Maybe that would be my catharsis. The only reason I left the house that summer, was for a French class; otherwise, I wouldn't have spoken to anyone.

I started considering transferring to Government Law College (GLC). I wasn't sure why. Maybe being back in Mumbai would change something. I missed my city, its haunts, the places I could disappear into. I didn't particularly enjoy hostel life. But mostly, I had started to realize that ILS wasn't going to give me what I was looking for. There were books, there were movies, things to get by on, but I didn't feel like I was moving forward.

My marks weren't good enough to get into GLC, so the decision was made for me. I braced myself for another year in Pune. But somehow, journalists got wind of my application.

Law college says no to Karkare's son, read a headline in DNA[21].

'Karkare's son, Aakash, graduated this year with 78% marks in BCom,' the article began, incorrectly, as always.

'The Karkare family did not approach anyone in the police force or the government to secure admission for Aakash,' it continued, as if this were remarkable. The education minister even wrote a letter to GLC, calling my case a 'special situation'.

There was even an element of intrigue: 'According to college sources, top cop Rakesh Maria's son was the only VVIP candidate to find a place in the merit list. Two other top-level officers got their sons admitted by pulling strings, though none of their wards scored more than 65%.'

I read the headline twice, feeling my stomach sink. I hadn't even wanted admission that badly, only applied to see if I could get in. But now, thanks to a news cycle I had no control over, I was in the middle of a controversy.

Mostly, I felt resigned. It seemed to be happening to another Aakash, a version of me that existed only in newsprint and on television. But I was also embarrassed, people were reading about me. People at college would see it.

The worst part was that the unwanted attention actually worked. I was offered admission. I went to GLC to fill out the paperwork. But when I stepped into the classroom, everyone turned to stare. I had no desire to start over again.

I walked out, caught the first train from Churchgate to Dadar.

Whatever ILS was, at least in Pune, it was my escape.

---

[21]Kolhatkar, Neeta, 'Law college says no to Karkare's son', *dnaindia.com*, 19 November 2013, https://tinyurl.com/yx7k7zmt. Accessed on 16 December 2024.

2

Some hope

The bus ride from Mumbai to Pune at the start of my second year was, without a doubt, the worst of my life, even worse than the one I'd taken as a child when the VCR broke and the whole bus groaned about not having a movie to watch.

The brief hope of GLC had only made ILS feel more like a trap. The thought of returning filled me with unbearable dread. I wanted to jump out of the bus, vanish into the middle of nowhere, find some tiny village between Mumbai and Pune, work on a farm, and never come back.

My desire to escape had reached absurd heights.

'You're back? Weren't you supposed to be in GLC?' a senior who never wore a shirt asked as I walked through the corridors.

How did he know? I hadn't told anyone.

Oh, right. People did read newspapers.

I nodded.

He began hanging around me for a few days, asking about 26/11 and my father.

'Why did all three of them travel together?'

'Did the government give compensation?'

Oh God, not this again. How could he not see how insensitive this was? He was making me relive my father's death all over again. But then I looked at his face, there was no malice, just idle curiosity. A kind of stupidity. He was like a character from an R.K. Narayan novel. Eccentric and nosy. A YD, waiting to repeat a semester before he could graduate, and in the meantime, he was looking for a bride. The dowry he'd get, he said, would fund his master's degree in the UK.

Somehow, my second year felt easier. I was settling in. We had moved up to the first floor of A Block in the hostel. We still shared rooms, but now we were all packed together, one after the other, side by side.

On my first night back, without thinking too much about it, I had my first drink, vodka with Sprite. The party picked up when a guy who loved to drink joined in, forcing shots on everyone, chased down with Coke.

'The bucket is over there,' someone muttered as another guy lurched forward and vomited into it.

The bucket was at my feet. Some of it splashed on my legs.

I guess my college experience was beginning a year late. We began hanging out often, eating meals together. It started to feel like a strange kind of family. I had stopped going to the mess quite early in the year, after people mocked me for being a spoiled kid from Mumbai. Slowly, one by one, others joined me. When the water ran out again that year, I didn't panic. I just went to the Café Coffee Day nearby to use their bathroom. I told myself my despair and alienation from the previous year had stemmed from too much free time. So I filled it. I joined a German class at Pune University, a harmonica class at a local music school, and began going to a local dive bar called Gautami. I didn't become an alcoholic, as my mother had warned I would.

I also started engaging in activities my peers pursued to boost their CVs: participating in Model United Nations (MUNs) and Moot Courts, applying for internships, and enrolling in diploma programmes in cyber law and human rights.

Once, I responded to an ad promising 'Work from home. ₹15,000 per month guaranteed,' only to end up at a conference comparing Sachin Tendulkar's and Shah Rukh Khan's endorsement deals as their way to get second incomes apart from their day jobs, suggesting we could earn similarly through a multi-level marketing scheme. I had hoped I might save enough to finance my own film, like the American independent filmmaker Richard Linklater, but it turned out to be a scam—5,000 rupees upfront for 'training', repayment promised once we started earning. Recognizing the pyramid scheme, I walked away.

All of this, I thought, would someday be material for a novel. I was merely collecting experiences. Still, I felt lonely. I'd spend long hours walking alone through Pune's streets, music in my ears, MP3 player in my pocket. I found it hard to connect with anyone beyond a certain point, but I was getting used to it. Someday, this would end. For now, this was my life, and I needed to be okay with it.

During the Diwali break, I landed an internship at a small family firm. Every day, I went around begging for work from the seniors. None of them seemed happy. I couldn't see myself becoming like them. I drafted contracts pulled from the internet, researched the Foreign Exchange Management Act for some cases, and sometimes bunked work to sit at Marine Drive all day. Mummy had saved my father's old clothes for exactly this reason. Unfortunately, they didn't fit me. When I told her to throw them out, she said, 'You can do that when I'm dead.' But she was happy to see me in formals, going to a law office.

'Your father would be proud of you,' she said.

During the last few weeks, the work dwindled to nothing when the depressed senior who'd been giving me assignments vanished on holiday.

One day, on the train home, I stood towering a foot above the crowd. From that vantage point, I noticed a middle-aged man in front of me. His face was etched with fatigue, dark bags under his eyes, tears brimming and catching the passing light through the barred windows, shimmering as they fell. In him, I saw my potential future. I imagined his past, perhaps once a boy contentedly digging in the dirt, now worn down by life's relentless grip, weeping on a train. That was when I decided I did not want to be a lawyer. Life was too fleeting, death too ever-present.

Over the summer, inspired by Christopher McCandless and

Werner Herzog, I decided to travel across India. My mother was in the US, and I had some money from the internship and what she had left me for emergencies. I went first to Delhi with S, staying at her friend's place for a few months. We spent time with her circle, some from JNU, others from the National School of Drama. For so long, I had felt like a lonely soul, convinced that the only people who thought like me, cared about what I cared about, lived only in movies or books or somewhere far away. I was too much of a misfit to belong anywhere I'd been.

For once, that feeling began to change. From Delhi, I went alone to Rishikesh, because I loved the mountains, and because the Beatles had once gone there. I spent my days walking around, sitting by the riverside, writing in my journal. Then I went to Mussoorie, drawn by Ruskin Bond's *A Room on the Roof,* which had been my favourite book alongside R.K. Narayan's *Swami and Friends.* I waited five days in Mussoorie just to get Ruskin Bond's signature; he came every Saturday to a local bookstore to sign books.

It was the first real vacation I had taken since 12th standard.

The first time I had left Maharashtra, I began to feel a strange joy and peace in anonymity. When I gave my surname and father's name to the hotel staff in Rishikesh and Mussoorie, there was no reaction. No one outside Mumbai or Maharashtra cared about my past. It felt like sweet relief. Maybe people were forgetting about it. I didn't have to be forever linked to a tragedy. I was ordinary.

'This is my favourite book,' I told Ruskin Bond when my turn came.

'How old are you?' he asked.

'Nineteen.'

'That's how old I was when I wrote the book,' he said. 'Who should I make it out to?'

'Aakash.'

'One A or two A's,' he enquired further.

A man after my own heart.

For aesthetic reasons, I always liked my name spelled with two A's. I loved how the double A looked. Unfortunately, when my father got my passport made, he used a single A, and I was forced to carry that 'incorrect' spelling on all my documents.

'Two A's,' I said.

It was not much of an interaction. Not the kind in movies or books where a huge revelation takes place, but it felt grand to me nonetheless.

Werner Herzog always wrote about adventure. Inspired, I decided to travel by bus from Mussoorie to Kanyakumari. From the North to the South. I thought nineteen was too young to spend five days in each place, travelling like an old person. So I kept moving. I returned to Delhi by State Bus, then went to Jaipur, where I stayed a day and walked around in the hot April sun, before continuing on to Jodhpur, and then Surat.

In Surat, I had planned to explore the city and try its famous non-vegetarian street food, but exhaustion overtook me. I passed out in a hotel room instead.

My journey wasn't grand like the one in *Into the Wild*, but it got me out of my head. It filled me with electricity and adrenaline. Those long hours on the road, staring at the scenery rolling past, Mussoorie to Delhi to Jaipur to Surat, across four states, made me alive to the vastness of India, to the possibility that countless stories existed outside of me. For once, I wasn't living inside my own head. That three-week adventure gave me a respite I hadn't found in Pune.

I returned to Mumbai intending to continue my travels South after a short break at home, but I never resumed the journey.

'You went straight from your room to around the country,' Kiran Mama said in astonishment.

Upon returning to Mumbai, I attended several theatre workshops. They made me happier than I had ever been in the past three years. Suddenly, the world felt brighter, sunnier. I no longer had to pretend I wanted to be a lawyer or cared about internships. I could admit, to others and to myself, that I wanted to act or write, and not feel foolish. Once I opened up about my struggles, I discovered others grappling with their own crises, engineers and MBAs questioning the careers they had pursued too. Being amongst them gave me joy. If even those who had chosen India's 'optimal path' were unhappy, then maybe I wasn't so lost after all.

In June, I travelled again, this time to Bihar with S who had recently finished her Masters and was back from Germany. For years, we had been receiving an email titled 'Hard Work No Pay.' Curious, I spent a week auditing the NREGA for a local organization. There was corruption, and things were poorly run, but there was also hope and idealism: people fighting for their rights. Even there, conversations about my father came up, but I didn't mind so much. Another awkward college student from Kerala asked, 'What was your father?' All I could do was nod, find it faintly funny, and change the subject.

When I returned to Mumbai, I knew I couldn't go back to ILS and ruin that state of mind. My admission at GLC was still technically open; the administrators had told me they didn't strike my name off the rolls for five years. My decision was made. I would return to GLC, where attendance wasn't mandatory, and spend the rest of my time on creative pursuits. The first time, I had left GLC because I was exhausted, unready. This time, I was going back because it was the only way to live on my terms. Without mandatory attendance, I could finally focus on what I wanted to do. Perhaps I should have switched degrees altogether, but it felt absurd to abandon my bachelor's when I was just a year away from finishing.

Meanwhile, S had secured funding from the Tata Institute of Social Sciences for a documentary about reading spaces in Mumbai, and she hired me as assistant director. Together, we made short satirical videos about life in the city. I directed a play with S as the lead at a theatre festival at NCPA. Naseeruddin Shah happened to be in the audience. He didn't say anything, but the mere fact that he was there made me feel as if all my dreams were coming true.

Once, while S, some friends and I were rehearsing improv in a park near our home in Dadar TT, Mummy driving by must have spotted us. Soon after, S's phone buzzed.

'Pappa would not like what you are doing,' Mummy had messaged her.

Those creative dreams began to feel infected with anxiety. Mummy started yelling, shouting, berating us like she used to. Maybe Pappa wouldn't have approved, I thought. But so what? Why couldn't Mummy support us? There was no point arguing anymore. I had to live for myself.

Two months after I transferred to GLC, the formalities still weren't complete. Every week, between French classes at Alliance Française in Cuffe Parade, I went to the college office, only to be told that something was missing. Fear crept in. What if I lost the year? What if I couldn't graduate? Even an artist needs a Bachelor's degree.

Four months later, my admission process was still incomplete.

After the 26/11 attacks, the government had announced a scheme for the children of martyrs, offering free education until graduation. The law school fee was only 15,000 rupees, and we didn't need the financial help. But on the morning of my admission, my mother convinced me to tell the college office about the scheme.

'It's a gift from your father,' she said. 'It will bring you good luck.'

Reluctantly, I handed over the announcement of the scheme. That single decision caused months of chaos. The policy had been announced, but no procedure had been put in place. The clerk looked puzzled; she had never heard of it. She said she would enquire and get back to me. Every time I followed up, she told me to wait another week. Sometimes, she even suggested it might block my admission altogether.

By the time the first-term exams arrived, I still didn't have an ID card. I decided to take both term exams together at the end of the year, a common practice in law schools.

I kept myself busy. I continued editing the documentary at the Tata Institute of Social Sciences, took improv and capoeira classes, and tried to write scripts and screenplays. But I couldn't recapture the happiness I had felt in my first few weeks after moving to Mumbai. I made endless trips to Mantralaya, Old Customs House, Mumbai University. Each office sent me to another.

I couldn't tell my mother. She had never approved of my decision to move to GLC, convinced that I 'never went to college.' Besides she would get stressed about such academic troubles for days, lose sleep and work herself into knots. She used to say '*Maze pay vakde zale*' (My legs have gone crooked) whenever such things happened. I wanted to spare her that.

Then the college asked me to prove I was related to my father. Fair enough, I thought. Then they asked me to prove that my father was the same person who had died during 26/11. I handed them a copy of the Ashoka Chakra citation.

'I'll just pay the fees,' I said. 'I don't need to avail of the scheme.'

'Now we can't take your money,' they replied. 'What if the government gets angry that we ignored their policy?'

The absurdity was inescapable. I had spent the past two years trying to carve out a life separate from my past, and now, for six months, that past was all I was forced to confront. That year, the college administrators and the guy who ran the Xerox shop outside, became my best friends.

Slowly, my brain rewired itself. I could only think about documents. Whether my admission was complete. Whether

I'd be allowed to sit for exams. Whether my life was on track, or whether I was about to become a wastrel lying in a ditch somewhere. I told myself I'd read the books I wanted to read, watch the films I wanted to watch, write the things I wanted to write, *once this was over.* Once my admission was finally sorted, I would have a calm mind. For the first time, art was of no use.

Then, without my knowing, all my struggles turned up in *The Times of India*, in an article titled: '*26/11 Mumbai terror-hit youngsters want to join the system to beat it.*'

'Psychiatrists say these tender minds have been branded by the scars of the tragedy that unfolded live on television,' a clinical psychologist explained. 'They have sublimated their childhood desires towards higher goals.'

'Akash has decided to fight for morality (right and wrong).'

'Klinger says they want to be part of law enforcement because they have been part of its failure. Psychiatrist Anjali Chabbra says, 'Young teens often want to be superheroes, they want to save the world. It is admirable how these children have channelized their anger in a positive way. They must have a sensible adult leading them through rational thought.'

'All those who watched the youngest child of the Karkare family, Akash, holding up his mother and two sisters during the public condolence and the subsequent funeral saw fury simmering in the 17-year-old. Today, the tall, broad-shouldered lad is studying in the third year in Government Law College, Mumbai.'

'Did you tell them this? Everyone in ILS knows I hate law and I don't like law school. They'll think I lied to the newspapers to make myself sound good.'

'I had no idea about this article. The author kept asking to talk to you, but I said you didn't want to.'

Then Mummy gave me her phone. 'Look she even sent me an angry message.'

The message, written without capitals or punctuation, said

she was very disappointed my mother hadn't helped her with the article after all she had done for us.

I began to furiously write a response.

'What are you doing?'

'I am going to tell this woman how unethical it is to invent an entire article. An entire story about me.'

'Don't do that.'

'I'll sign my name.'

'We might need her help.'

I paused. I looked at my mother and didn't know what to say anymore.

For years, I had resented her for giving interviews, for keeping us tethered to the past. But now I saw the other side. She didn't have the option to disappear. I had youth on my side. She had responsibilities, expectations, a life redefined without her choosing. I wanted her to escape, but she couldn't. And I didn't know what to do about that.

I eventually sat for my exams in October of the following year. I had done what my mother feared most, lost a year. And she didn't even know it.

Today, when I look back on that two-year period, I am ashamed. I could have avoided so much by making better, more informed decisions. But that's the tragedy of life: hindsight always makes it clearer where you went wrong. It was best not to dwell on it.

3

Living the dream

As what should have been the final semester of my fourth year came to a close, I applied to several journalism institutes across India. I wanted to sharpen my writing, and maybe even explore filmmaking. For the first quarter of 2013, I reported on the ATP Tour for a sports website. A year of making short films, followed by four months of writing, had given me a solid portfolio.

I got into three institutes. The Asian College of Journalism (ACJ), in Chennai, cost four lakh rupees, and going there meant telling my mother. Sophia Institute in Mumbai was half the cost. ACJ topped the *Outlook* rankings; Sophia didn't feature in any. But it had Jerry Pinto and P. Sainath. I remembered transcribing S's interview with Pinto for our documentary *Books in the Big City* and being struck by his clarity on life and art. 'The only reason to write a book,' he said, 'is if it's stuck in your throat, begging to come out.'

I borrowed money from S for a laptop and the fees and began the diploma.

After five years of doing what I didn't want to, I was finally studying what I did—film theory, filmmaking, photography, journalism—subjects I had already explored on my own while studying law. There were still things I didn't care for, like PR and advertising, but that didn't matter. For the first time in years, I felt like I belonged. The cynicism that had settled in me began to lift. I was less angry, more optimistic. Studying at a college in South Mumbai had always been a dream. Now it was real. My future, once muddied, was beginning to clear. I could finally see a light at the end of the tunnel.

That's when I met K.

We lived close by and started splitting taxi rides to college. Trains were faster and cheaper, but I had a crush on her and wanted the extra time together. I didn't say anything. Back in 11th standard, I'd told a girl I liked her and she never responded, killing the friendship entirely. I was still stung from that, too afraid to take another chance.

K and I bonded over books, a mutual friend, and the coincidence of growing up ten minutes from each other. We joked about the tiny store called Asian, with its sign: *We have everything. Don't hesitate to ask.* We laughed about the eccentric family who ran the local Irani store. We shared our fondness for Guru Kripa samosas, which always tasted best cold, once the oil had fully soaked through.

The next day, I was too embarrassed by how much I'd revealed to even look at her.

At some point, I told her not to Google me.

'Why?' she asked.

Then she held my hand, and googled me.

There were the photos, ones I'd seen years ago, once on my own, and once again in the ILS hostel, when some classmates had googled each other for fun. None of them had results. I had stayed silent, hoping they wouldn't search me. They did. The images from my father's funeral surfaced immediately. To cut the tension, one guy joked, 'Hey Aakash, why are there topless photos of you on the internet?'

K studied them quietly.

'You look like a kid,' she said. 'You look so afraid. I can't look at it.'

No one had ever given me that kind of understanding before. It made me want to cry.

The relationship became addictive. We spent most of our time together. We both wanted to be artists. We both wanted something different. It was my first relationship. The first time I fell in love. The first time I felt like I had something close to a family. Someone who knew me. Someone I wasn't afraid of.

By the end of August, we had said we loved each other.

We shared everything: books, food, cooking, art. We created our own world. We told each other we'd never have relationships like our parents, full of taunts and simmering resentment. I had always been a romantic, falling for manic pixie dream girls in movies. But when I showed K *Eternal Sunshine of the Spotless Mind* and *Before Sunset*, she was bored. She wasn't a manic pixie dream girl. She was real.

My assignments now involved writing scripts, essays on world cinema, documentaries. One of our films was screened at Tata Lit Live. I even taught a class at St. Xavier's on Expressionism, thanks to S. One problem remained: Mummy didn't know. She still thought I was in my final year of law school. Only S knew the truth. One evening, while I was with K, I got a message from Mummy:

'You are studying at Sophia's?'

I panicked.

'What happened?' K asked.

I told her. She found it both hilarious and unbelievable.

'How can a mother not know where her son studies for six months?'

Mummy had found out at a *satsang*, where she met a classmate's mother.

'Why didn't you tell me?'

'You were too busy giving interviews.'

'How will you make money in the media?'

'I'll find a way.'

Eventually, we reached a compromise: I could finish the diploma, pursue media work if I wanted, but I would also return to GLC and complete the law degree. A fallback plan, for her peace of mind.

26/11 still had strange ways of resurfacing.

The fifth anniversary was approaching. One of the professors called me into the staff room to discuss whether it would be okay for the journalism teacher to assign 26/11 as the final project. I said it was fine, but I wouldn't be able to participate. Thankfully, it didn't happen.

In the middle of the course, I dislocated my shoulder. As I was being wheeled out of the hospital after surgery, my mother asked, 'Did you tell a journalist that you didn't want Kasab hanged?'

'No,' I said.

The only time I'd spoken about the subject was during the ACJ interview, when a professor from *The Hindu* asked about my thoughts on capital punishment. I had simply said I didn't believe the state should have the right to take life.

Besides that, there were few reminders. I barely thought about our past anymore. It only seemed to exist in other people's memories.

When the course ended, I took a job at a production company. It paid 25,000 rupees, a good starting salary, and got me out of the house. I didn't particularly want to do it, but I had heard this was how filmmaking careers began: start in production, learn the ropes, then transition into film. GLC didn't require attendance, so I could continue with the law degree on the side.

On my first day, the accounting guy taking my details asked, 'You're Hemant Karkare's son, right? The boss told me.'

For a moment, I wondered if I'd been hired because my father was dead. I put the thought away, like I did with most things related to his public life. A month into my probation, I realized I didn't care for the job. It wasn't satisfying, and I didn't care about selling Pepsi.

One day, I was sent to a dentist's office on Yari Road with a child actor, to get her teeth fixed for a commercial. I was instructed to haggle with the dentist for a discount. Sitting there, arguing about a child's tooth, I thought: *I'm a graduate. This is not what I trained for.*

The next day, to my boss's annoyance, I quit.

By the time my fourth year at GLC began, I'd started working with a documentary filmmaker on a film about India's feminist movement, profiling Majlis, a legal centre founded by the activist and lawyer Flavia Agnes. I read more legal documents during that project than I ever had in law school. Mornings were for lectures. Afternoons and evenings, I transcribed interviews, went on shoots, sat in on edits. At night, K and I went for movies, art exhibitions, long walks, and to our neighbourhood bar, New Punjab. She had begun a master's in English at Mumbai University.

I was building the life I wanted, one I'd dreamed of since I was seventeen. For the first time, I wasn't looking for an escape.

Background Noise: Headlines from 2009 to 2014

'If nobody was at fault, I would not have lost my husband'[22]

'Why Maria didn't know where Karkare was on terror night'[23]

'Senior officers don't even look at intelligence reports: 26/11 Panel'[24]

'I did speak to Karkare: Digvijay'[25]

'I have never made false or untruthful statement in my life: Digvijaya Singh'[26]

'Digvijay Singh wonders why his statements trigger controversy'[27]

'Bullets did not pierce Karkare's bulletproof vest: Post-Mortem Report'[28]

'Theft complaint on bulletproof jacket'[29]

---

[22]Staff reporter, 'If nobody was at fault, I would not have lost my husband', *mumbaimirror.indiatimes.com*, 29 May 2009, https://tinyurl.com/6e86n6dc. Accessed on 16 December 2024

[23]Staff reporter, 'Why Maria didn't know where Karkare was on terror night', *mumbaimirror.indiatimes.com*, 28 November 2009, https://tinyurl.com/bdhttnxt. Accessed on 16 December 2024.

[24]Staff reporter, 'Senior officers don't even look at intelligence reports: 26/11 panel', *mumbaimirror.indiatimes.com*, 2 December 2009, https://tinyurl.com/h5tvnnfd. Accessed on 16 December 2024

[25]*PTI*, 'I did speak to Karkare: Digvijay', *thehindu.com*, updated 17 November 2021, https://tinyurl.com/5fj6wd24. Accessed on 16 December 2024.

[26]*PTI*, 'I have never made false or untruthful statement in my life: Digvijaya Singh', *economictimes.indiatimes.com*, 6 November 2011, https://tinyurl.com/2b7x78e8. Accessed on 16 December 2024

[27]*PTI*, 'Digvijay Singh wonders why his statements trigger controversy', *economictimes.indiatimes.com*, last updated 6 November 2011, https://tinyurl.com/42brfvrb. Accessed on 16 December 2024.

[28]*PTI*, 'Bullets did not pierce Karkare's bullet-proof vest: Post mortem report', *timesofindia.indiatimes.com*, 21 November 2009, https://tinyurl.com/ysu62xte. Accessed on 16 December 2024.

[29]Hafeez, Mateen/*TNN*, 'Theft complaint on Karkare jacket', *timesofindia.indiatimes.com*, 17 November 2009, https://tinyurl.com/2pw8jenz. Accessed on 16 December 2024.

'Court asks State to reply to allegations over substandard bulletproof jackets'[30]

'Karkare death not due to faulty jacket'[31]

'BMC dreads hunt for Hemant Karkare's vest at Deonar dump'[32]

'Karkare's jacket wasn't good enough, cops admit in court'[33]

'Probe sought in Karkare's death'[34]

'SC pulls up RSS chief for his remark on Hemant Karkare'[35]

'Malegaon road named after Karkare'[36]

'Maharashtra ex-IGP says IG got Karkare killed'[37]

'Why Karkare family's NOC needed to set up NGO in his name'[38]

---

[30]*Mumbai Mirror*, 'Court asks State to reply to allegations over substandard bulletproof jackets for cops', *mumbaimirror.indiatimes.com*, 11 December 2009, https://tinyurl.com/mr2a7k4r. Accessed on 16 December 2024.

[31]Ali, S. Ahmed/*TNN*, 'Karkare death not due to faulty jacket', *timesofindia.indiatimes.com*, 21 November 2009, https://tinyurl.com/4w3jz5x4. Accessed on 16 December 2024.

[32]Desai, Geeta, 'BMC dreads hunt for Hemant Karkare's vest at Deonar dump', *mumbaimirror.indiatimes.com*, 26 December 2009, https://tinyurl.com/3szjkeew. Accessed on 16 December 2024.

[33]*Mumbai Mirror*, 'Karkare's jacket wasn't good enough, cops admit in court', *mumbaimirror.indiatimes.com*, 1 April 2010, https://tinyurl.com/mrych3yt. Accessed on 16 December 2024.

[34]*TNN*, 'Probe sought into Karkare's death', *timesofindia.indiatimes.com*, 18 August 2010, https://tinyurl.com/3dhubsmd. Accessed on 16 December 2024.

[35]Agencies, 'SC pulls up RSS chief for his remark on Hemant Karkare', *indianexpress.com*, 29 February 2012, https://tinyurl.com/2vvwt74x. Accessed on 16 December 2024.

[36]Hafeez, Mateen/*TNN*, 'Malegaon road named after Karkare', *timesofindia.indiatimes.com*, 17 September 2010, https://tinyurl.com/3xh6babv. Accessed on 16 December 2024.

[37]Bose, Soumittra S/*TNN*, 'Maharashtra Ex-IGP says IB got Karkare killed', *timesofindia.indiatimes.com*, 4 January 2010, https://tinyurl.com/4r9fwmxv. Accessed on 16 December 2024.

[38]*PTI*, 'Why Karkare family's NOC needed to set up NGO in his name', *economictimes.indiatimes.com*, last updated 10 February 2013, https://tinyurl.com/4y79nb2z. Accessed on 16 December 2024.

Part III

A Complete Set

(2013–16)

'The ceiling fell out of my life. When you complete the set, the floor goes with it, now you have nowhere to go, neither up nor down, nothing to fight against. When you lose someone who helped form you in a lot of ways, who is your 'true north,' you lose the barometer of your life. You're no longer trying to please someone, or you're no longer reacting against something. In many ways, you're truly alone.'

—David Fincher

1

Severance from the past

September 2014

It was time for me to get ready for class. I needed to catch the 7.10 fast train to Churchgate. I usually didn't pay much attention to attendance, but you never know when it might suddenly become mandatory. Instead, I was still in bed, too lazy to move, lost in *The Incal* by Alejandro Jodorowsky— one of the greatest sci-fi comics ever to be written—reading it on my mother's iPad, which she rarely used.

The air was still cool from the previous night's air conditioning. Just as I decided to get comfortable and bunk my lectures for the day, there was a knock on the door. Maybe Mummy wanted me to hurry up. That would be odd; she usually never interfered with these things. My eyes were half closed when the knocking grew frantic. I quickly pulled on a T-shirt and shorts before opening the door.

It was Lata Bai. Her face looked ashen.

'I've been knocking for so long,' she'd said.

I was still half-asleep, unable to process what was happening.

I followed her to the living room. Mummy was lying on our decade-old, light-brown sofa darkened with years of use. She was on her side, eyes half open.

'Mummy,' I'd whispered softly. Then louder.

'She screamed loudly and fell to her side.'

'Is she breathing?' I'd asked.

Lata Bai looked at me in confusion. I'd forgotten the Marathi word for 'breathe'. Only *jeevant*, alive, came to mind, and I didn't want to go there. I pressed my ear to Mummy's chest but felt nothing. I checked her wrist, but the pulse felt too faint. Should we start CPR, I'd wondered.

The doorbell rang. It was Kiran Mama. Lata Bai had called him from the landline because I wasn't opening the door. Together with one of the armed guards outside our bedroom window, Kiran Mama and I carried Mummy to the still-running Fiat parked at the front gates of European Quarters.

'I got a taxi, an ambulance would take too long,' Kiran Mama informed me.

I'd nodded and squeezed into the front seat, my head hitting the roof. Kiran Mama sat in the back, next to my unconscious mother. I didn't know what to think anymore.

The taxi sped over Tilak Bridge, past huge red trucks loaded with fresh produce for the vegetable *mandis*, wholesale markets. Morning walkers in tracksuits were on their way to Shivaji Park. I looked back at Mummy, still unmoving. Kiran Mama stared out of the window. I wondered if we were thinking the same thing.

Mummy often told the story of how her father had died when she was twenty. He had been a fit, able policeman and had had an aneurysm on the badminton court. She never seemed to have gotten over that loss. He was her best friend, the only one who didn't favour her brothers over her, unlike her mother.

At Hinduja Hospital in Mahim, only ten minutes away, Kiran Mama rushed in to fetch a stretcher and nurses. I waited by the taxi. Mummy was still in her favourite maroon dressing gown, stained by several years of use and always smelling of her.

They wheeled her in to the ICU. The doctors told us to wait outside. One handed Kiran Mama a form. He quickly pushed it towards me. 'I can't do all this,' he'd muttered, looking away.

Of all things, I remembered the Hindi film *Munna Bhai M.B.B.S.*, the scene where Sanjay Dutt berates the hospital for making relatives fill forms before admitting patients. Even in emergencies. The doctors here felt just as detached, cool, almost nonchalant. I didn't know what to make of it.

I began filling the form in my messy handwriting that both my parents always hated. My eyes blurred as I wrote: *Name of Patient: Kavita Hemant Karkare. Cause of Admission: Loss of Consciousness.* I blinked and a tear rolled down my cheek.

I looked up and saw my neighbour. He had arrived shortly after us. He looked impassive. Didn't say much. Only looked at me for a while. I was always uncomfortable showing emotions.

'My parents died when I was a young boy too,' he'd said and then had proceeded to sit down next to me.

I liked his matter-of-fact treatment of death. Still, even the second time around, I felt numb. It seemed unreal that less than an hour ago, Mummy was on the sofa, eating *ghavan*, a Maharashtrian rice pancake that I never really liked.

'Do you want to eat with me?' she had asked as I rushed past after my shower. I'd refused. Her lifelong wish was to have the five of us sit for dinner together. 'You three wastrels will only eat dinner together on the day of my funeral,' she often said to J, S and me.

Now, my uncle began calling the extended family. Kakas, Kakus, Mamas, Mamis, people I hadn't spoken to since Pappa's death. People I had no desire to see again. I tried WhatsApp calling S in Colorado, but it was past 1 a.m. there. No answer. Finally, I texted: *We are orphans.*

I scrolled through my contacts, considering calling K but she must have been sleeping too. So I sent her a text message explaining what had happened.

The relatives arrived. Familiar faces, familiar expressions. They hovered, waiting for something to say. A touch on my shoulder. Someone murmured, 'So sorry, *beta*.'

It was all the same as last time.

The wives of officers came in. They said 'sorry.'

I nodded.

I couldn't bring myself to go through these rituals a second time.

'So Aakash, are you in the fourth year of law or the fifth? Shouldn't you be finishing by now?' One of my eccentric mamas had asked.

'This is not the time to get gossip about my education situation,' I wanted to snap, but instead I nodded, got up, and told Kiran Mama I was going home. The neurologist had said they needed to wait for the pressure in Mummy's head to go down before a scan could confirm anything.

'What are the odds of her waking up again?' I'd asked.

'Not good,' one neurologist had told me.

'Could we have done anything else? Brought her to the hospital sooner?'

'All of us carry aneurysms that could rupture at any time,' he'd replied. 'The best time for intervention was days or weeks ago.'

The previous evening, Mummy had come home from office and repeated a ritual she'd carried out her whole life, asking '*Konacha fon bin?*' (Did anyone call?) as she kicked off her sandals.

On the way home, Mummy's phone rang, which I was carrying in my pocket.

'Hello, Kavita,' a woman spoke on the phone.

'It's Aakash,' I'd replied. 'Her son.'

'Oh, I am calling from her college. She's late. When will she come today? Class began fifteen minutes ago.'

'She's in the hospital. She's unconscious,' I told them.

I was unable to use words like 'aneurysm' and 'haemorrhage'.

'Oh. Okay. Keep us updated.'

Back home, I lay on the bed, staring at the ceiling, unable to believe what had happened in just a few hours. My phone vibrated. It was K. I told her everything. She listened quietly. I was afraid of burdening her. Our relationship was only a year old. She told me to come over.

Her sister and some friends were in the living room, so we went into her bedroom and lay down. She held me. And suddenly, just as when Pappa died, rage began to tumble out.

'I can't do this again,' I'd whispered.

K kept stroking my back, her breathing even. She didn't really say anything.

'I won't,' I'd said, louder now. 'Not the funeral. Not the media. Not the pity. I won't.'

By the time Mummy died, my relationship with her, like with Pappa, had become almost non-existent. We were living separate lives, in different worlds. It felt as though the relationship had ended long before her life actually did. I realized that the numbness that followed their deaths came from this simple truth: there wasn't much of a relationship left. And what was there was filled with pain and anger.

At some point I fell asleep. Over the weekend, the neurologists confirmed that my mother was brain-dead. Now the decision had to be made, whether to take her off life support.

'Do you want to donate her organs?' they asked me.

'We will have to wait for my sisters to arrive.'

The hospital slowly began to buzz with people. The police had, once again, become involved. My mother and I had a joint account, and when I went to pay the bill at the reception, they told me the police would take care of it. I should've felt grateful, I suppose, but instead, I was afraid. Life had conditioned me to believe that any favour came with an expectation of repayment.

I spent most of my time away from the hospital and home. K and I sat at Carter Road, staring at the sea. There wasn't much to say. I kept hoping everything would soon blow over. By Monday, my sisters arrived. Together, we told the doctors to take Mummy off life support. We agreed to donate her organs. The hospital staff asked if they could release this information to the media. Journalists had been calling all morning. I looked at my sisters, then shook my head.

'We want privacy,' I'd said.

'But they are calling again and again,' the hospital's PR lady told us. She seemed to have an air of excitement about her. As if she was eager to talk to the media about an important death in their hospital. The wife of martyr Hemant Karkare.

They eventually released a statement. Was the circus going to begin again?

Soon after that, I stepped out of Hinduja Hospital to make a phone call and caught a flash in the distance. A shifty-looking man was holding a camera. I stared at him, growing angrier by the second. Marching up to him, I demanded that he delete the photo. I had never done anything like that before, but now that I was an orphan, I wanted to reclaim some agency over my life, even in the smallest possible way.

'You have my word,' he told me. 'I have already deleted it.'

I didn't really believe him. I considered asking him to show me, but decided that being the kind of person who lied about such things was punishment enough. As I turned back toward the hospital, another journalist sidled up beside me. They seemed to be hiding everywhere.

'What do you have to say, Aakash?'

'I don't want to say anything.'

I was about to walk in the hospital when she said, 'We have done so much for your family.'

I wasn't personally aware of what they had done. I turned to look at her. She looked so young, barely out of her teens. I felt a surge of anger but couldn't tell at whom: the journalists swarming us, the circumstances themselves, or simply the fact that both my parents were gone and I didn't know how to process it. Without another word, I stepped inside.

The next morning, the *Mumbai Mirror* screamed: 'Second Tragedy in Karkare Family in Six Years.' On page two, next to the article, was a grainy photo of me. Why would anyone want to see what a son looks like after his mother has died? And if they did,

did that curiosity really need to be indulged? Would people stop picking up newspapers on their commute if there weren't at least one tragedy to consume?

The articles were riddled with errors. *Mumbai Mirror* reports: *'Karkare was a professor at a B.Ed. college in Mumbai, but had stopped working in the recent past,'* and *'Akash is pursuing his five-year law course in Pune.'* The mistake about my mother was particularly infuriating. Not only did they freeze her forever as a 'widow' in the public eye, they added the lie that she had quit her job, just to make her death sound even more tragic. For days, even people who saw me regularly, like the staff at my physiotherapist, asked me when I returned from Pune.

The Hindu[39] ran an obituary: *'Ms. Karkare, 57, was a professor at a B.Ed. college in Mumbai but has stopped work recently.'* Incorrect again.

The *Economic Times*[40] peculiarly referred to her by her first name: *'Kavita has been vocal about the security lapses that she feels facilitated the terror attack and contributed to the death of her husband in an ambush by terrorists in South Mumbai on the night of November 26, 2008. She had also been demanding better weapons, training and facilities for police personnel after her husband's killing.'*

NDTV reported: *'Her body will be donated for medical research.'* [41]

The *News Minute*[42] adds: *'She leaves behind two daughters who have decided to donate their mother's organs.'*

[39]Staff reporter, '26/11 hero Hemant Karkare's wife dies of brain haemorrhage', *thehindu.com*, last updated 31 July 2016, https://tinyurl.com/48ss3fcf. Accessed on 16 December 2024.

[40]*PTI*, 'Kavita Karkare, widow of 26/11 hero Hemant Karkare, dead', *economictimes.indiatimes.com*, 29 September 2014, https://tinyurl.com/3nnnya4f. Accessed on 16 December 2024.

[41] NDTV, 'Kavita Karkare, Wife of Top Cop Killed in 26/11, Dies in Mumbai',ndtv.com, 29 September 2014, https://tinyurl.com/5dxyfzyn. Accessed on 16 December 2014.

[42]*TNM*, 'Kavita Karkare, wife of slain ATS chief Hemant Karkare is no more', *thenewsminute.com*, 25 February 2015, https://tinyurl.com/v47zykbv. Accessed on 16 December 2024.

When I returned home from the hospital, J was furious. A man had come by, claiming to be a close friend of a family friend, and asked for Mummy's eyes for his blind wife. 'I am not a dealer of my mother's organs,' she'd snapped.

I was angry too. Then I found it absurdly funny. Then I started feeling sorry for the man. And finally, I was furious all over again, this time at the journalists. The following day, we discovered through the papers who had received her organs. One of them even wanted to meet us. Wasn't the entire point of organ donation anonymity?

All this made me determined to keep the funeral as quiet and private as possible. An electric furnace over a grand wooden pyre. No government officials. No media. A few days earlier, an argument with my uncle about the funeral arrangements had convinced me to take charge myself. The more people got involved, the further I felt from the rituals of grieving. My sister S and I went to the markets in Dadar West to buy the items needed for the funeral: the bamboo, the white sheet, the coconuts. I didn't believe in any of it personally, but Mummy did. This, I told myself, would be the last religious ceremony I would ever take part in.

'Can you ask people from the police force not to come?' I had asked Mr Padsalgikar, one of my father's colleagues, when he had called to ask if we needed anything.

'How can I do that?' he replied.

'I just want it to be a private, family affair,' I'd said.

I wanted to avoid the pageantry that had accompanied my father's funeral. The memories still felt like deep wounds. I could still picture a man's hand, holding a TV camera high over the mossy, dust-stained wall of our apartment complex to capture a shot of my father's dead body on the stage the police had erected. I instantly recalled that woman who, after claiming relationships with a string of people I could not even place, had asked me for a sound bite.

I was just as angry as I had been back then. Time had not healed much.

Three days after Mummy's death, I sat dazed inside the ambulance leaving Hinduja Hospital in Mumbai's Mahim West. It was 7 a.m. and the light filtering in through the van's rear windshield was grey and dull. I wasn't fully awake. We passed Shivaji Park in Dadar West, but it felt like half an hour had passed while we had barely moved 350 metres. The ambulance was crawling so slowly, it seemed almost stationary. Leaning forward, I peered through the windshield to see what could possibly be causing traffic in a residential neighbourhood long before rush hour. In the distance, a policeman on a government-issued black TVS motorcycle was moving so slowly he needed to balance himself with one foot on the ground.

'He's doing it intentionally,' I muttered to no one in particular, furious.

'Perhaps it's for safety,' my kaka offered.

But all I wanted was for the funeral rituals to be over. The longer they took, the more time I had to spend inside this frozen, clenched numbness. As the twenty-minute ride stretched into an hour, numbness turned to irritation, irritation blossomed into rage. We crawled past Siddhivinayak Temple, then through Worli Naka, the officer still riding slower than I had ever seen anyone ride. Instead of thinking about Mummy, or the fact that I was now an orphan, the authorities had once again managed to taint another memory with white-hot anger. They were never going to let me grieve in peace.

At the crematorium, my uncle and I moved the stretcher into the furnace, and the door shut with a clang. He burst into tears. I couldn't cry, not because I didn't want to, but because in the first days of death, when you are consumed by death certificates, forms, and endless tasks, your emotional self simply shuts down.

One by one, relatives and friends of my mother walked past, offering their condolences. I nodded mechanically. J sobbed beside me, and my mami leaned over to console her. I felt deeply uncomfortable with most Hindu rituals of death. They seemed to prolong suffering, yet at the same time they were necessary. They forced you to confront the worst parts of death, the stark, biological reality of it.

As I left, a man arrived in a white Indigo with a red beacon on top. Dressed in a police uniform, he walked over, shook my hand, offered his condolences, and departed just as quickly. I didn't know who he was. Later, I realized that he, or one of the other officials at my mother's funeral, must have been responsible for the ambulance delay on the way to the crematorium. Perhaps they couldn't make it that early in the morning and sent a junior to slow down the ambulance carrying my kaka, my mama, my mother's body, and me.

I lowered my head as the Swift Dzire, my mother's recent purchase because it was one of the few cars that could fit my 6-foot-6 frame, carried my sisters and me home. I wanted to avoid the cameramen from local news channels. Still, I felt a quiet relief. It was the last time I'd have to endure all of that.

Journalists from NDTV keep calling for interviews until my eldest sister eventually agreed. Barkha Dutt asked the questions, and to me, they seemed particularly designed to elicit emotions so she'd get the money shot: the tears of an orphan.

'Amazing parents, though children seem less than keen to talk about the past. Natural, I think,' she tweeted later.[43]

How could she know what they were like as parents? Why did it matter to her whether we chose to speak or not? And what did one have to do with the other?

It didn't matter. As long as I never spoke about it again, as long as I avoided policemen, the government, and journalists, no one else could speak for me.

Every connection to the past had been severed by then.

---

[43]Dutt, Barkha, *X* (formerly *Twitter*), 14 October 2014, https://tinyurl.com/y9n9h5vu. Accessed on 16 December 2024.

2

Moving out

Mummy and I were supposed to begin moving out of European Quarters, because Pappa, had he been alive, would have turned sixty in December and retired.

In October, I was meant to be sitting for my fourth-year mid-terms at GLC. The documentary on Flavia Agnes, which I had been researching for months, was finally scheduled to begin shooting. But both were put on hold. I deferred my exams to the next semester, unable to manage the demands of academic deadlines, film work, and the logistics of relocating. I was preparing to move into a small apartment in nearby Hindu Colony, a place that would soon become my home, but at the time, was in disrepair and badly in need of renovation.

My mother had begun making preparations for the move back in September, albeit with a lot of apprehension. Moving out meant severing all links with the last remnants of my father.

'Why don't you take the UPSC and become an officer like Pappa?' She'd often joke, half-serious, half in hope.

I looked forward to the move. European Quarters had always felt like a favour, something begrudgingly extended to us. Mummy often told S and me how the women from the IPS Officers Wives Association would ask pointedly how much longer we planned to stay.

'It's none of your business,' Mummy finally snapped at one of them. After that, she never went back.

In all, we ended up living in Dadar TT for fourteen years. Eight of those in European Quarters. Most of the deaths in my family had taken place there: Pappa, Mummy, and Bombay Aaji.

Even Lata Bai, our house help, said she was afraid to come inside. To her, it seemed cursed.

Mementos of those past lives continued to exist as I began to live by myself in that apartment. There was the Sony Bravia television that had been purchased for my grandmother for her to watch her favourite Marathi TV show, an upgrade from our Onida television. In the Diwali vacations during my second year of college, I'd asked Bombay Aaji what was happening in those shows. She'd said, 'I've stopped watching them. Have no interest in them.'

What she really meant was that she had lost interest in living. A few months later, she got a cough that never stopped, and she passed away at eighty-six. I didn't go to her funeral; everyone else was grieving, but I disagreed with that. We should have been celebrating the long, full life she had lived.

There was also the centre of the living room, where my father's cold body, wrapped in a blue sheet, had lain almost six years earlier. The sofa with the broken spring, where everyone sank to the middle, was the same one my mother had sat on for her last breakfast, before collapsing with a scream I never heard.

The back garden, which my father had created a few years before his death when he suddenly developed an interest in gardening, still stood. The rocking chair he'd bought for my mother on my sister's suggestion remained too. Even the false ceilings with their peculiar finish, adored by my father but disliked by the rest of us, reminded me of him. My dislike was less aesthetic and more practical: being on the ground floor meant constant battles with insects, lizards, and sometimes rats. The false ceiling was a perfect haven for them.

Over the years, as we carved out separate rooms and even converted dining spaces into bedrooms, we accumulated three air conditioners for the three people in the house. Two of the LG window units had followed us from house to house, and were over a decade old. The third, a new Lloyd, had been bought for my mother after she finally conceded that Mumbai summers were too hot even for her.

'Soon, like J and S, I am going to move out,' I told her once. 'Then you will be a lonely woman with three ACs.'

She'd clapped her hands together in glee and laughed uproariously.

'Maybe you could use that image as the opening of your memoir,' I'd added. Sometimes I'd try to get her to write. I thought maybe we could be writers together, somehow bridging the huge gap that had developed between us.

This is how we communicated in our family, through humour and black comedy. Humour saved me from the grimness of death. After my parents died, it lingered. We had been a family of five, now reduced to three.

'And then there were three,' J, S and I joked, drawing an eerie similarity to the situation in Agatha Christie's mystery novel.

But in the end, it wasn't my mother who became the lonely one with three ACs.

It was me.

In her version of the ending, I imagined a happy old woman with glasses hanging from a string, someone who had finally learnt to enjoy life after 'two-thirds of it were over,' as my mother often liked to say about her fifties. In my version, I found myself twisting and turning in bed at night, sometimes hearing my mother's voice call my name, days, weeks, even months after she had died. In the mornings, I went to banks, and the offices of insurance agents, to wrap up the affairs of my dead parents, and in the afternoons, I tried to study for my law exams, but the words refused to stay. By night, sleep eluded me entirely. They were all out to get me. Someone. Anyone.

Each night, just as my head touched the pillow, just after I had put away whatever I was reading, when sleep's tendrils tightened around my brain, my mouth grew dry, and my eyes drooped shut, I would think I heard a thud at the door. Or the doorbell ring. Or a whisper outside my window. Instantly, I would enact a home-invasion scenario in my mind and jolt myself awake.

I couldn't understand where the fear was coming from. I lived surrounded by police officers. Not even the most incompetent thief would dare to strike here. Research reassured me that Mumbai had very few cases of home invasions, and my neighbourhood was considered one of the safest in the city. But there was a caveat: my home was on the ground floor of a two-storey building, tucked into a lane just off an arterial road, one of the busiest in the city, a road infamous for its traffic jams. Thousands passed by each day; not all of them knew that these hundred-year-old buildings housed police families.

One of the countless cars going past my home could easily carry thieves. Thieves who could jump over the boundary wall and find their way into my home. My only source of protection was a flimsy plywood door, unchanged since long before we moved in, its only renewal the coat of white paint applied each Diwali. Even locked, it would give way with a single shove.

If a thief broke in and found nothing valuable, he might turn violent. We would scuffle, and, since this was the house of the dead, the odds were stacked against me. Perhaps another scenario: the intruder's noise would wake me, and blinking eyes in the dark would be the last thing I saw.

The scenarios would become ever more frightening as the night progressed. They would be imbued with elements from all the movies and television shows I had seen, news reports and crime scene investigations on broadcast news, the countless thriller books I had read, cases I had overheard my father discuss. Every time I was about to sleep, a police siren seemed to ring out in the distance, images of blood leaking out onto the white tiles flashed in my mind, spreading all over the floor in an ever-widening stream.

I would try to reason with myself in the dead of night. I

didn't possess anything worth stealing, save for a three-year-old MacBook Pro for film editing; a garden variety Samsung phone; a six-year-old Sony Bravia television I almost never used, and some silver utensils of my mother's that I kept forgetting to put in a bank locker. I never kept more than a few thousand rupees of cash at home. None of these arguments proved sufficient in the middle of the night and sleep refused to come.

At last, around 5 a.m., I would drift into fitful rest. By then, neighbours were awake, and I told myself no thief would be foolish enough to rob a house in broad daylight. And if he did, I could call upon the newspaperman, the milkman, or even the man who left flowers at the door.

I wanted life to return to normal. I didn't have many friends, and I avoided meeting people, afraid they'd ask about Mummy, about what it felt like to have dead parents, about how I was coping. K and I resumed spending time together. I began transcribing interviews for the documentary and attending shoots within weeks. But however hard I tried, the nighttime fear never lost its grip.

I decided that I needed a game plan for me to fall asleep before dawn. I was going to move out of my bedroom, which sat by the front door, and into S's old room, buffered by two doors and a passage. There were two routes from the main entrance to her room. The first passed through mine, then my mother's, into the passage, and finally to this one. I locked both doors of my room and the connecting door from my mother's. Three layers of security. The second route led from the entrance into the living room, which also opened into the passage. I locked both living room doors and the entrance to the room I was sleeping in.

Satisfied that the fortress was secure, I hunkered down on a bed far too small for my six-foot-six frame. The window above my head opened into the courtyard, where the staff quarters stood. If intruders came, I could shout for help.

The guards who had patrolled European Quarters since

Pappa's death left the day after Mummy's passing. Had I grown subconsciously dependent on their presence? Though I was almost relieved when they came to say goodbye, I now wondered if their absence was what had set my fear loose.

One afternoon, a grocery delivery man arrived with an order I hadn't placed. He was certain 'Aunty' had called it in. I almost snapped, ready to tell him 'Aunty died a month ago,' but stopped. Some small, fearful part of me worried that revealing the truth would expose the house as home to a lonely orphan. Thankfully, a neighbour stepped out and took the delivery. Only later did I realize why the mix-up had happened, the landmark given must have been 'opposite Karkare's home.'

It wasn't the first time. Each time I ordered food, the delivery men asked for a landmark. I offered vague ones, near the train station, near Tilak Bridge, but avoided the one name that would ensure swift delivery.

'Near Karkare's home?' he asked.

'Yes,' I responded. 'Karkare's home.'

Regretting the decision to order food, I hung up.

Aha, I thought. I have found the true cause of my suffering. Too many people knew whose house this was. Which meant they then knew an orphan was in their midst. I removed the name plate from the front door.

I had a thousand explanations for what was happening to me. But not the one that mattered. Anything but grief. Anything but that.

One night at 2 a.m., in a state of panic after running through my usual home invasion scenarios, I walked to the kitchen for water. A shadow on top of the fridge caught my eye, a hook-like shape, coiled like a cobra. 'Don't be stupid,' I told myself, but fear overtook me. I couldn't bring myself to turn on the light. What if it really was a snake? I shut the kitchen door and backed away, heart pounding. I tried to distract myself but couldn't shake the thought. Staying home felt unbearable. I grabbed my car keys and drove, blasting music, speeding down Palm Beach Road in Navi Mumbai at 120, maybe 160, km/h. By dawn, exhaustion replaced fear, and I returned home, ready to confront reality.

I crept to the kitchen, flicked on the light, and looked up. The 'snake' was a black polythene bag, one handle sticking up, containing grapes I'd forgotten to refrigerate. I laughed, ate a few, and fell asleep instantly. If only I had put the grapes away like a responsible adult, I could have saved myself a night of paranoia. What else could I do save eat a grape and go to sleep?

That should have been funny. It was for a while. And the next morning, I felt light. *But how had my own mind betrayed me like this?*

'The house eats you,' a relative once told me. I hadn't believed him then, didn't want to believe him at all. I was a strong, twenty-three-year-old man. I would live alone and prove everyone wrong. Some had even suggested I move in with them, or let them move in with me. Thankfully, those nightmares never come to pass.

Most of my relatives were conservative, traditional, often right-wing. One of the few strange consolations in the death of your parents is the severance it brings, the clean break from the past. Besides, I didn't think it was normal for a grown man to be looked after by others.

By February 2015, it was time to move to the new home. The newest of the three AC units had broken, while the other two were being serviced before installation in the apartment. The gaping holes above the windows were stuffed with sheets of newspaper. That last week in European Quarters was its own particular hell. Every night, I imagined someone vaulting the wall and slipping in through the gaps. On the few nights K stayed over, the fear disappeared.

The final drive to the new home took place in my mother's Swift Dzire. I loaded my father's police uniform and paraphernalia into the trunk. Then I got into the car, took a long, deep breath, and glanced at European Quarters on my right.

I couldn't decide whether to feel sad about leaving the family home or happy that, in some twisted way, I was getting what I had always wanted: moving out of the government-given European Quarters. There was no cinematic moment of looking back one last time. Just relief, total, unambiguous relief.

3

Moving on

Mummy had saved Pappa's clothes for my wedding or for some future job at a big corporation. These suits and shirts, remnants of his bureaucratic and police career, didn't fit me.

'What do people do with all these things? What are they supposed to do?' K asked once, when she came over as I was packing up all the belongings in European Quarters.

'I guess you take them out once a year, look at them while drinking a glass of whisky, and have yourself a good old cry,' I replied.

If life were a postcolonial novel, I would have done just that. Instead, I donated them to a children's shelter. I called a scrap dealer to take away all the showpieces, old bedsheets, knick-knacks, and 'future-use' items Mummy-Pappa, both lifelong hoarders, had collected. When I die, I thought, I want to leave behind as little as possible. Nothing for the next generation to sort and pack.

I decided that the new home in Hindu Colony had to be a fresh start. Moving on and healing were not just things inside our head. They were also actual steps you had to take. Objects themselves could weigh you down.

Since the flat had become infested with termites, I hired a contractor to tear down all the built-in furniture: the showcase for Pappa's knick-knacks from around the world, a plywood partition, and every last cupboard and cabinet. When it came time to paint, I turned to K for help.

'I'm hiring you as the designer,' I joked. She loved this sort of thing and readily agreed. We had both grown up in middle-class homes stripped of colour, so together we staged a rebellion: painting the kitchen a bright yellow, the study a parrot green, and the largest wall in the living room a deep navy blue.

It was a rebellion, a rejection of the past. A declaration that Mummy was no longer around to insist on beige, and that I would be okay with it. K and I would build a new life here. I would overwrite the sad memories of my childhood with happier ones from my twenties.

Some things, of course, I hadn't been able to throw away. Not out of sentimentality, I told myself, but because some objects felt immovable. Steel Godrej cupboards were priceless, teak furniture was sacred, and I had no interest in defying those lessons just yet. So my parents' old bed and its ornate floral side tables were kept in the unused guest room. I retained a colonial-era study table, even though I no longer fit it, and the six-seater dining table, though most meals were eaten alone, or, at most, with one other person.

My new bedroom housed the steel Godrej cupboard from my old room in European Quarters, freshly painted blue to banish its usual rusty grey. I bought a new double bed. As for photographs, I decided only the good memories deserved a place here. I framed old pictures of my parents from Chandrapur, during Pappa's posting, and others from when I was a baby, S six, J ten.

I also replaced the front door with a double door fitted with the latest lock technology, which the contractor assured me was impenetrable. A few months later, when I locked myself out without a key, a lockmaker popped it open in seconds. 'For real security, you need a digital lock,' he advised. I worried about safety, but not enough to spend 25,000 rupees on a new system after just shelling out 16,000 rupees on this one.

I, who had been a lifelong shy kid, had been forced to come out of my shell and negotiate with all these professionals. It somehow calmed me. They operated firmly on the material plane. Their world was simple: a problem, a solution, a fee. They made life feel manageable. I had to learn how to run a house on my own. For a while, Lata Bai and Sangeeta continued working here until a new officer's posting took up their time. I used their departure as an opportunity to let go of the middle-class habit of underpaid domestic help, a system I had always been uneasy with. The result was a house blanketed in a thin film of dust, and a fridge filled with rotting produce because I hadn't yet mastered shopping for one. The online grocery apps, still in their infancy, rarely offered quantities smaller than 500 grams, too much for a single person. But this was my dust, my filth. The early hiccups of learning to live alone.

And yet, for the first few months, I was blissfully relaxed. From the vantage point outside my bedroom door I could see the entire house. With everything moved in, there were no hidden nooks and crannies with hidden objects, no sudden memories waiting to ambush me. The huge windows let sunlight flood across white tiled floors, bright and easy to clean. Most importantly, I now lived on the sixth floor of an apartment building, with a security guard downstairs. I felt safe. For the first time in a long time, I could sleep at night.

I had put most of my life on hold for this move. I should have started studying for my fourth year at GLC, but that had been a promise to my mother, one I no longer had to keep. I couldn't summon the energy to study for exams I didn't want to take, for a profession I had no interest in. I worked on the documentary in bursts, but just as I was about to commit full-time, the funding collapsed, as is common in the Indian independent documentary scene. Majlis, the organization we were filming with, disbanded. Just like that, the project was over before it had properly begun.

It felt strangely freeing that I had no one to ask for advice. I had no plan, no roadmap, but maybe that was okay. Still, I found it puzzling whether I should be grieving in a way that matched other people's expectations.

'I was shocked,' friend after friend told me the first time we met after Mummy's death. 'It's fine,' I'd say, wanting to avoid the subject, wanting to ease their awkwardness as much as mine. Then I'd add, 'She had hypertension and diabetes,' as though the true tragedy was that it had been shocking.

When I turned to Google, my generation's method of seeking advice, I discovered that other orphans described something similar. After the initial shock of losing their parents, some felt not happiness, but a kind of release. The fear of disappointing someone was gone. The ever-present voice telling them what to do, or what not to do, had vanished. It wasn't joy, exactly, but it was close to lightness. The constant echo of doubt and criticism in their minds, the echo of a parent, was gone. The past no longer pressed down on every decision about the future. For many, it was unexpectedly liberating.

My eventual goal was to either be a writer or filmmaker, but Werner Herzog once said in a talk for his Rogue Film School that a true artist must have real experience. So in the first months of 2015, I went for as many interviews as I could. Several led to offers, but something always stopped me from taking a full-time job.

The writer Jerry Pinto, who had been my professor in college, had once told me after class, 'Aakash, you will never be able to work in an office.' At first, I was offended. Later, I realized he had only said what I already knew. I had grown suspicious of institutions, and the office was just one of them. Another professor, who wanted me to pursue documentary films, mocked me when I mentioned working in advertising. So I avoided the well-paying PR jobs and instead took smaller gigs, often barely paid, sometimes only after repeated reminders. This was a luxury I could afford, since I didn't have to pay rent in Mumbai and had an inheritance to fall back on.

That summer, I began working as a photographer for a book on the history of Mumbai through its architecture. Every morning in May 2015, I woke at 5 a.m., got into the Swift Dzire, and drove across the city: to the heritage buildings of South Mumbai, the Mandapeshwar and Mahakali caves in the suburbs, the forts of Kalyan, Worli, and Sion. By night, I was brimming with images of Mumbai's diversity, unable to make sense of it all. I devoured every book on the city I could find. After years of hating Mumbai, I was slowly beginning to fall back in love with it. Much of my relationship with K was intertwined with this rediscovery of the city.

I wanted to go to every inch of the city, every locked door, uncover every hidden truth. The only way to do this was through journalism. Yet, I'd always been afraid that I'd be made to interview someone who'd gone through something similar to what I had, and I wouldn't be able to say no; or that I'd find myself in the shoes of Soha Ali Khan in *Mumbai Meri Jaan*, covering an anniversary of 26/11 and find myself unable to say anything through my tears. So I chose the next closest thing: writing ad copy for *Architectural Digest*. My sole reason was that its office was in Ballard Estate, the historic district modelled on London's business quarter, and that the job would last only six weeks. It was my first time working in an office since Mummy's death. I was nervous, as I always was in new social settings, but especially so because I hadn't yet learnt how to talk about my parents' deaths. I would have preferred never to have the conversation at all, but work didn't allow that. My revelation was always followed by a long, melancholy 'ooh', an up-down nod, eyes cast downward, a silence I rushed to break with a quick change of subject. These events would take place at strange moments.

Once, during a debate over the meaning of a Marathi word, my boss suggested I ask my mother to settle the matter. Four or five smiling faces looked at me, coffee cups in hand. It wasn't the moment to say, 'That will be difficult. My mother is dead.'

I let it pass. But soon it compounded. A few days later, the same colleague, noticing I ate lunch at a nearby Irani café every day, said, 'Why don't you ask your mother to pack you a dabba? You'll fall sick otherwise.'

By then, I had lied by omission. If I confessed now, it would seem strange, even duplicitous. So the silence continued. Sometimes I wondered if, when people eventually found out, I would appear as some kind of double agent, deceitful by default. But avoiding awkwardness always won out.

Even strangers stumbled into it. One of the office staff, standing beside me at the urinals, asked, 'You're Karkare right?'

I nodded.

'We should talk about it sometime,' he continued.

I nodded, zipped up and left.

Gradually, more people knew. A friend of S joined *Condé Nast Traveller* just as my six-week project extended into another. By the time 26 November arrived, word had spread. A colleague I had never spoken to before came up to me and asked quietly, 'You're Hemant Karkare's son, right?'

I nodded awkwardly, once again.

'Thank you to your family,' he added, shook my hand, and walked away.

My first instinct was always to check if anyone around me had noticed, but they didn't seem to have. I suppose I could have taken it as a mark of pride, but I always found it profoundly embarrassing.

The past had begun to resurface in strange ways. Walking through the neighbourhood, I'd catch residents staring, whispering as I passed: *'Don't you know him? He's the boy whose dad got shot.'*

It wasn't easy to hide. I looked almost exactly like my mother, and I was probably the tallest person in the neighbourhood. People would stop to shake my hand. Delivery men saluted me and asked how I was coping after my mother's death, which they'd read about in the papers. Even the men installing my Wi-Fi asked for a selfie. I refused.

What do you do when, after a long, sweaty wait at a government office, your turn at the counter turns into the day's spectacle because your full name gets recognized on the documents?

'Come see,' they'd say at the Aadhaar office, the electricity department when I went to inquire about the unreasonably high power bill, or the pension office. 'This is Karkare's son.'

'Didn't you get your father's posting?' Adult men and women who had MBAs would ask in the offices of banks and insurance companies. 'Why don't you become a police officer?'

They probably thought reality was much like a Bollywood film.

Once, a shifty-looking man in the neighbourhood who was always seen near burning stacks of paper, came over to me, shook my hand and then nodded to someone in the distance as if letting that person know that he knew me. For days, I wondered if I was about to be pulled into some scam.

After Mummy's death, my phone number replaced hers as the contact for strangers. Journalists called for comments on the latest 26/11 updates. Organizations wanted to me to hand out bravery awards on Independence Day. The police invited me to appear in a National Anthem music video to be played before film screenings.

'I'm busy,' I said.

'Think about it,' the officer replied. 'Even Farhan Akhtar is going to be part of it.'

It never seemed to occur to people that badgering the son of someone murdered nearly six years ago might be cruel. Every year, as the anniversary approached, old friends and complete strangers slid into my Facebook DMs. Law school classmates hoping to enter politics reappeared. Former media colleagues contacted me for film rights, patriotism and nationalism were in fashion, and stories like mine would be easily greenlit.

Once, I tried to be honest. A cop came inviting me to a flag-hoisting on January 26th, and I told him it was too painful. I even used the Marathi word *vedana*, grief, agony, hence would not be able to attend. He was the Matunga Mill Special, he said, someone who went undercover during labour movements when mill workers had been protesting. He first ignored this blatant show of emotion and then tried to make a joke of it, but I desisted. He nodded, left, and a few months later, something else happened, and once again the police were at my front door, calling me incessantly.

I wondered if I would ever be able to leave the past behind. Maybe I should leave India forever. Maybe I should change my surname.

'Maybe you should write to Google,' K suggested, 'and tell them to delete all the photos of you.'

I considered it. But I was also defiant. This was my city. My home. My country. My surname. I would not give those up because of what other people projected onto me.

Apart from these constant reminders of the past, there were others, the kind that appear when parents die suddenly. Pappa had once allowed a neighbour to park his car a few feet into our spot because of a leaking sewage pipe. When I moved back in, I knew nothing of this arrangement. The watchman always stopped me short of the wall when parking, and I thought nothing of it, until one resident, who disliked the neighbour, told me the entire space belonged to me and urged me to park against the wall. So I did. What followed was a fiasco, alternately absurd and panic-inducing, dredging up the same night terrors I'd carried from European Quarters.

The neighbour above, a powerful builder with political ties, sent a police officer to interrogate me in my home about the parking spot. By then, all family secrets had died with Mummy and Pappa. I didn't care about the space and would have gladly given up the few feet, but the building was divided into factions, and I didn't want enemies. So I stayed quiet. One resident even suggested leaking the matter to the local press: *How could anyone take away the parking space of Karkare's son?*

'Those facts have nothing to do with one another,' I said. 'Please, let's not do that.'

The cold war over parking dragged on for most of 2015. I began to feel genuine fear after reading reports of powerful builders embroiled in violence, how people in Mumbai had killed one another over parking disputes. Eventually, the matter was resolved when the building secretary, an airline employee, brought in a cartographer and official land records from the BMC to map out the space. The neighbour everyone despised has been arguing over one square foot of parking space..

These were the strange lessons of adulthood. Blackly comic, but also alienating. When I went out for drinks with peers, they discussed the usual things twenty-somethings talked about. Meanwhile, I was juggling parking disputes and court cases.

Mummy had once given our MHADA flat in Versova to a tenant recommended by one of Pappa's colleagues. After her death, the tenant stopped paying rent and even demanded a 10,000-rupee reduction. I had no idea about the arrangement, but I had just read Voltaire's *Candide* and was determined not to be taken advantage of. I refused. He promptly filed a case in Small Causes Court. So in between working at *Architectural Digest* and trying to run a home, I found myself travelling to Bandra for court appearance, because my lawyer was always too busy to go themselves.

The rent was 30,000 rupees, but Mummy had increased it by 5,000. 'She died because she made me pay more,' the tenant said over the phone when I yelled at him for not paying.

What could I say to that?

'Didn't people kill one another over such disputes?' I thought to myself.

The court case eventually ended, because I, tired of the never-ending pattern of court dates, and the arguments with the tenant,

I'd acquiesced to all of his demands as long as he vacated the premises after a year. I lost a couple of lakhs in the process.

It was a peculiar time. Some days, life felt good. Things clicked into place, and I didn't imagine I'd be killed in my own bed. As time passed, the good days slowly outnumbered the bad. In the rhythm of daily life, my anxieties rarely surfaced. It was as if I had split into two selves: the one who functioned by day, and the other who unravelled by night. Perhaps this, I thought, was just adulthood. In the daylight, the whole thing felt faintly surreal, almost absurd. I viewed my own life from a distance, as though it were material for a novel, and I was merely a detached observer watching the show unfold.

Most times the show seemed funny. I only wished sometimes that playing my part was easier.

4

Ghosts of my mind

One night, I jolted awake, convinced I'd seen a laser sight fixed to my forehead, followed by the click of a trigger. When I woke up in the dark bedroom drenched in sweat, there was no one there.

I couldn't understand why this was still happening, why the nightmares continued nearly two years after my mother's death. It had been almost eight years since 2008. I didn't remember being such an obsessive worrier before. Was it because I had never resolved any of the mysteries of my past? Was I up late at night worried about intruders to my home because I had never gotten that much depicted emotion in art and cinema: catharsis?

I did what I had long avoided: I plunged down the rabbit hole of the 26/11 case, poring over reports, testimonies, and court records. I had never truly investigated what had happened that night. The details seemed to exist around me, ambient and unresolved, something even my mother had once articulated.

'I just didn't know anything in the initial six months,' she had told *Rediff* in 2009.[44] 'Politicians, the media, and others came to see me, but I was not aware of what exactly was going on. No senior officers told me what had happened with my husband. I've only gathered information from the media, from magazines and newspapers. Till date, I don't know the exact facts about that day.'

Over the years, layers of obfuscation and hearsay had so thoroughly clouded the truth that I began to believe I'd never

---

[44] *ANI*, 'Karkare and others did not get backup for 40 minutes: Kavita', *rediff.com*, last updated 18 November 2009, https://tinyurl.com/3x6bd4nw. Accessed on 16 December 2024.

really know what happened. Maybe it was better that way. I told myself not to go down the dark corridors of the Indian Deep State and global terror. What would be the point? I could indulge conspiracy theories when they involved other people. I loved gossip like anyone else. But when it came to Pappa, it was different. The darkness wasn't abstract. It was personal. And I didn't want to confront what that might mean.

Still, as the night continued to be a place filled with ghosts I turned to a Google search.

Around 11.30 p.m., my father, along with four other officers, had reached Cama Hospital following the trajectory of the attack where Sadanand Date had been in a gun battle with Kasab. The Mumbai Police Headquarters was only a few kilometres away, and my father, 'codenamed Victor' on the police's wireless channel made an urgent request for backup so that the hospital could be encircled and the terrorists could be prevented from escaping. The support team did not arrive in time, while Kasab and Ismail walked out of the front entrance and ambushed the Toyota Qualis in which my father was sitting. The bulletproof jacket, which my mother later called a 'baby frock' in interviews, was of no use.

Why the police had not sent help in time, and why they had allowed people to believe that my father and his fellow officers had rushed in recklessly, remained a mystery best left to the police to answer.

The Mumbai Police would later argue that since the five bullets that killed my father had pierced his shoulder blade and neck, even a good bulletproof jacket would not have saved him. Yet, they never explained why substandard jackets had been purchased in the first place, especially after the officer vetting them had noted that they could not even withstand 7.62 mm self-loading rifles.[45]

[45] Ali, S. Ahmed/*TNN*, 'Karkare death not due to faulty jacket', *timesofindia.indiatimes.com*, 21 November 2009, https://tinyurl.com/4w3jz5x4. Accessed on 16 December 2024.

Even as my father was wheeled into JJ Hospital, the bulletproof jacket had gone missing.[46]

My mother had filed a Right to Information application in 2009 and received the reply that the bulletproof jacket my father had worn had been missing.[47]

'When his body was found, the bulletproof jacket was missing…even at the hospital,' she told *The Times of India*. 'TV channel recording clearly shows Hemant wearing a jacket at CST and leaving in the van. Where did the jacket go? I do not know if someone took it from him after that or it was removed from his body later, but it is missing…'

That same year, the Maharashtra Chief Minister, Ashok Chavan, ordered a probe[48] into the faulty jackets and vowed to 'find the truth'. Maharashtra Home Minister, R.R. Patil, too, had ordered a probe.[49] Another social activist had filed an FIR about the issue.[50]

In response to the FIR, a sweeper at JJ Hospital claimed to have disposed the bulletproof jacket in a dustbin.[51] 'On the night of November 27, after Karkare's body was brought to JJ Hospital for autopsy, I had mistakenly put the jacket along with bio-medical and non-medical waste in polythene bags which was

---

[46]Dutt, Barkha, *This Unquiet Land: Stories from India's Fault Lines*, Aleph Book Company, New Delhi, pp. 85–87.

[47]*PTI*, 'Wife files RTI over Karkare's missing bulletproof jacket', *timesofindia.indiatimes.com*, 11 November 2011, https://tinyurl.com/42epuf7v. Accessed on 16 December 2024.

[48]Agencies, '26/11 fallout: Chavan orders probe on faulty bullet-proof jackets', *indianexpress.com*, 14 November 2009, https://tinyurl.com/yxks6nd6. Accessed on 16 December 2024.

[49]*PTI*, 'R R Patil orders probe into Karkare's "missing" jacket', *timesofindia.indiatimes.com*, 28 November 2009, https://tinyurl.com/yfyrtzmx. Accessed on 16 December 2024.

[50]*PTI*, HT Correspondent, 'FIR in Karkare's missing jacket case', *hindustantimes.com*, 8 December 2009, https://tinyurl.com/sndfz7mz. Accessed on 16 December 2024

[51]*PTI*, 'Hospital sweeper claims he disposed off Karkare's missing bulletproof jacket', *timesofindia.indiatimes*.com, 23 December 2009, https://tinyurl.com/5n85nx2k. Accessed on 16 December 2024.

sent to the Deonar dumping grounds for disposal,' he said in a statement.

'I have lost all hopes to get fair justice in this case. I do not believe in this,' my mother responded in the same article. 'The government is under pressure and hence this statement at this late juncture.'

The mystery would be 'solved' a year later when the Mumbai Police responded to another RTI. The bulletproof jacket had, indeed, been disposed of in a dustbin.[52] The police department had known of this lapse in 2009 but had chosen to keep mum.

The story of the bulletproof jacket seemed particularly odd and unbelievable. Why would they have removed it while wheeling my father into the hospital? How could a sweeper have simply disposed of such an object? It seemed far more likely that the Mumbai Police wanted to sweep under the rug the fact that they had failed to protect my father from the terrorists' bullets. After all, just a year earlier, public prosecutor Ujjwal Nikam had admitted that the widely repeated story of Kasab being served biryani in prison was a fabrication, concocted to sway public sentiment.[53]

What else had the government, political figures, legal establishment, and the police lied about? What else had they invented?

S.M. Mushrif, a former Intelligence officer, had authored the book *Who Killed Karkare* in 2010. Until then, I had avoided it. I remembered when a copy arrived in the mail for my mother, the cover bore my father's face alongside a title that felt sensational, even exploitative. I had assumed the author had written it as a shameless cash grab. But this time, I began to wonder if there

---

[52]Sayed, Nazia, and Anupam Dasgupta, 'Bulletproof jacket that failed to protect Karkare dumped in dustbin: RTI', *mumbaimirror.indiatimes.com*, 25 June 2017, https://tinyurl.com/2k2p79xc. Accessed on 16 December 2024.

[53]*PTI*, 'Kasab never asked for biryani, we fabricated it, public prosecutor Ujjwal Nikam says', *timesofindia.indiatimes.com*, 20 March 2015, https://tinyurl.com/mr2wpup6. Accessed on 16 December 2024.

was something to what he had been saying all those years ago. I purchased the two books he had written about 26/11—*Who Killed Karkare* and *Why the Judiciary Also Failed?*—bracing myself for confirmation of my worst fears.

Instead, I found the book shrill, angry, the voice of a lonely man shouting in the middle of the street. According to Mushrif, Kasab himself did not exist. 'Ballistic report proves that he was not killed by the bullets of any terrorist (who carried out the attacks),' he told *The Indian Express* around the time of the book's launch. 'I have a strong feeling that workers of Abhinav Bharat and some officials of the IB must have been involved in it. It should be investigated.'[54]

Adding, 'My book clearly exposed how IB conducted a parallel operation to eliminate Karkare in the lane of Rangbhavan.'[55]

The photo that had been shared in the news was a plant. He had accurately found all the loopholes. *Why was there a delay in providing backup? Why had three senior officers gone to Cama Hospital?* And promptly filled all those loopholes with conspiracy. I felt that believing in the things he believed in would make me become like him, so I stopped reading the book after a few pages.

Was there another way to uncover the mysteries of Pappa's death? Around this time, a Facebook post by Anand Patwardhan, the documentary filmmaker who had directed *Raam Ke Naam* and *Jai Bhim Comrade*, amongst others, caught my eye. He had used the term 'murdered' for my father, which I found odd. Did he subscribe to Mushrif's view too?

He had once come to my college for a talk and was widely admired in the documentary and journalist circles I moved in. I

---

[54]*Express News Service*, 'Ex-IG S M Mushrif, calls for banning RSS, questions IB', *indianexpress.com*, updated 24 February 2016, https://tinyurl.com/yyf9dwpt. Accessed on 16 December 2024.

[55]Bose, Soumittra S/*TNN*, 'Maharashtra ex-IGP says IB got Karkare killed', *timesofindia.indiatimes.com*, 4 January 2010, https://tinyurl.com/2b9uwwtv. Accessed on 16 December 2024.

admired the rationalism of his films and had always found them eye-opening. I wrote to him to ask why he had used the term 'murdered'. He invited me home, and to my surprise, I discovered he lived just a few feet away from European Quarters.

He showed me footage from the documentary he was shooting, *Reason*, which examined the killings of rationalists like Kalburgi, Dabholkar, and Pansare by lone gunmen affiliated with the Sanatan Sanstha. My father had first drafted a proposal to ban the organization in 2008.[56] He was featured in the documentary because Pansare had been shot a day after Mushrif had scheduled a talk in Pune to discuss his theories and his book, *Who Killed Karkare?* In the footage, Mushrif was framed against the wall, rambling about the case. None of what he said was substantiated or verified.

'Why now?' Patwardhan asked me.

I couldn't say it was because I was looking for catharsis and wanted to sleep.

'I've always wondered about it. Just thought you might know.'

'I believe sixty per cent of his theories,' Patwardhan said.

I didn't ask which sixty per cent.

'Do you have any papers at home which your father might have left?'

Not that I was aware of. I'd dumped all old photos and belongings of my parents inside a suitcase and under one of the beds but never opened them and had no plans to.

'I don't think he was aware it would become something like this.'

'All trust amongst Brahmins,' he said, laughing, a remark I didn't understand because Pappa was not someone who spoke about his caste like that.

'Your mother refused the one crore that Modi offered?'

---

[56]Hafeez, Mateen/*TNN*, 'State ATS had first sought ban on Sanstha eight years back', *timesofindia.indiatimes.com*, 12 June 2016, https://tinyurl.com/58cjtc98. Accessed on 16 December 2024.

I didn't reply. This was one fact only S and I seemed to know the truth about.

As I was leaving, we spoke about conspiracy theories in general. Patwardhan mentioned he believed 9/11 was an inside job, claiming the towers had fallen in a controlled demolition. I myself had subscribed to that view when I was ten, back in 2001. It had fuelled several drunken conversations with friends. But hadn't architects themselves confirmed there was no controlled demolition?

I no longer knew where to turn. There was no point in going further down this rabbit hole. Instead, I went back to an old quote by Alan Moore, the great writer of comics such as *Watchmen*, which had brought me comfort during such times:

'Yes, there is a conspiracy, indeed there are a great number of conspiracies, all tripping each other up,' he once said while talking about a book that explored conspiracy theories. 'The main thing I learned about conspiracy theories is that conspiracy theorists actually believe in the conspiracy because that is more comforting. The truth of the world is that it is chaotic. The truth is, it is not the Jewish banking conspiracy, or the grey aliens, or the twelve-foot reptiloids from another dimension that are in control. The truth is far more frightening: no one is in control. The world is rudderless.'

The theories about Pappa have continued into the present day.

'The matter is extremely serious,' Congress leader Shashi Tharoor said in 2024.[57] He was backing his party colleague, Vijay Wadettiwar, and Leader of the Opposition in the Maharashtra assembly. 'Our concern is that when the LoP points to something that is an allegation that has been in the public domain for some time and which featured in a book by the former IG of police, S.M. Mushrif, who said that the bullets found in Karkare's body

[57]*HT Newsdesk*, 'Shashi Tharoor backs Vijay Wadettiwar over Hemant Karkare remark, attacks Ujjwal Nikam', *hindustantimes.com*, 6 May 2024, https://tinyurl.com/3k9hkfye. Accessed on 16 December 2024.

could not have been fired by Ajmal Kasab and that it could have been fired by a police revolver.'

~

I stopped this descent into the dark corridors of the mind when I was hired by the news website *Scroll.in*. A few weeks into that job, the National Investigation Agency (NIA) dropped all charges against Pragya Singh Thakur and five others. Charges under the stringent Maharashtra Control of Organised Crime Act were also dropped against ten other accused, including Lt Col. Purohit.[58]

According to *Mumbai Mirror*, the chargesheet suggested that the investigation conducted by my father, then ATS chief, was 'flawed' because statements from the accused had been obtained 'under duress.' In April 2016, several witness statements recorded in the presence of a magistrate were declared missing, while others had been 'watered down.'

An official BJP spokesperson made the allegation that Pragya Singh Thakur had been framed. The Congress and CPM countered, accusing the ruling government of orchestrating this outcome to protect RSS[59] members, even dubbing the NIA the 'NaMo Investigation Agency.' The Shiv Sena 'hailed'[60] the acquittal of Sadhvi Pragya. The Aam Aadmi Party (AAP), through its member Ashish Khetan, questioned the credibility of the NIA, terming it a 'caged parrot.'[61]

---

[58]*Mumbai Mirror*, 'Pragya gets clean chit, 26/11 martyr Karkare discredited', *mumbaimirror.indiatimes.com*, 14 May 2016, https://tinyurl.com/2etrxrzd. Accessed on 16 December 2024.

[59]*TNN*, 'Malegaon blasts: NIA now Namo Investigation Agency', *timesofindia.indiatimes.com*, 14 May 2016, https://tinyurl.com/4978jvbm. Accessed on 16 December 2024.

[60]*PTI*, 'Shiv Sena hails acquittal of Sadhvi Pragya and others, professes demand of Hindu rashtra', *economictimes.indiatimes.com*, 16 May 2016, https://tinyurl.com/2ah3pxsz. Accessed on 16 December 2024.

[61]*PTI*, 'AAP questions NIA credibility in 2008 Malegoan blast case', *economictimes.indiatimes.com*, last updated 14 May 2016, https://tinyurl.com/2v5w74xa. Accessed on 16 December 2024.

Social activist and former IAS officer Harsh Mander had predicted this outcome a year earlier, after special public prosecutor Rohini Salian had been removed from the NIA's panel of lawyers. 'Ever since the tragic killing of Hemant Karkare during 26/11, very little credible evidence has been gathered by investigating agencies,' he said. Over the years, Salian had also noted that the only thing consistently discussed in the case was bail for the accused, who were Hindus.

Salian had revealed she was asked to 'go soft' in the Malegaon blast case after the National Democratic Alliance (NDA) came to power in 2014. The NIA responded to criticism that it was casting aspersions on my father's investigations, when he was no longer alive to defend himself, by saying that 'ATS shortcomings were not a reflection on Karkare.'[62]

'There's nothing in the chargesheet on him [Karkare],' an NIA officer told *The Times of India*. 'We detected shortcomings in the ATS probe, which we told the court.'

'We'll go by what the court says now,' NIA DG Sharad Kumar added. Despite the serious allegation made against an ATS officer for planting evidence, the NIA upheld the veracity of most of the case's evidence.

As usual, my phone, always on silent mode, began to buzz non-stop. It would ring until the end and then start again. I quickly finished writing all my articles for *Scroll* that day and then switched off my phone. When I turned it back on the next morning, there were several WhatsApp messages asking for comment. One, from a journalist at *The Indian Express* with a patronizing tone about the importance of speaking out, caught my eye. I Googled his name. He was around my age, maybe a year younger.

What did he know about what I'd been through? How dare he give me advice about speaking out when he was just twenty-three?

---

[62]Jain, Bharti/*TNN*, 'ATS shortcomings not a reflection on Karkare: NIA,' *timesofindia.indiatimes.com*, 14 May 2016, https://tinyurl.com/3as44byc. Accessed on 16 December 2024.

S forwarded me an email from another *Indian Express* journalist. It began with 'Ms Kalaskar', a portmanteau of the names Karkare and Salaskar, and asked for comment. The journalist added that if she didn't want to be named, they could use 'an unnamed family member' as the source. S and I discussed whether we should respond but eventually returned to our usual belief that there was no point. Even though I'd ignored most of the articles over the years, I'd still heard about them through countless sources. Anyone who had been on the Hemant Karkare beat as long as I had could have predicted the NIA's actions. If journalists were shocked by this revelation, it only meant they didn't really know anything.

Even so a few days later I asked Naresh Fernandes, the editor of *Scroll*, if we could speak privately. We went to the tiny terrace on the mezzanine roof of the Bandra bungalow that housed the office, where colleagues usually went for a smoke.

'Umm… I was wondering about my father,' I began.

'Yes, I can't imagine what you must be going through.'

'I was wondering if I could write something,' I said.

'What would you write?'

I hadn't given that aspect too much thought, but before I could say anything, Naresh added, 'It would be a conflict of interest.'

I nodded.

'If you have any papers at home that your father had left behind, they could be of help,' he continued, as I bent down under the small door to re-enter the office.

I agreed with his view. The NIA, and by extension, the NDA government, were besmirching my father's work. Family members should not be asked for comments. It was the duty of reporters and journalists to investigate the chargesheet and then debunk it.

Still, my father's old colleague Julio Ribeiro, whom my mother had once introduced me to at the wedding of a colleague's daughter, wrote a column in *The Indian Express*. It appeared in print under the headline 'Burying Karkare' and was later reposted online as 'Malegaon blasts case shows that Hindutva forces are succeeding in widening Hindu-Muslim divide.'[63]

Ribeiro, who knew my father well, wrote that he was one of the few remaining officers of integrity, 'both financial and intellectual.' He recalled that my father had visited him a day before his death, on 25 November, disturbed by L.K. Advani's accusation that the ATS had framed Pragya Thakur and others. My father had insisted he would never 'frame anyone' and had brought along case papers to prove the investigations that identified the real culprits. Unfortunately, Ribeiro had been too busy to review the documents then but assured my father that he would speak with Advani.

He went on to describe the decade-long pattern of the Malegaon blasts case. Initially, the ATS had arrested the 'usual suspects', but under my father, a more plausible group was apprehended, based on solid evidence, including phone intercepts. Later, the NIA weakened these charges instead of strengthening the case. Public prosecutor Rohini Salian's claim that the NIA had pressured her to go easy on the accused further indicated political interference. Ribeiro lamented that to achieve this, Karkare's reputation had been sacrificed.

Many officers expressed disappointment at the NIA's actions, suspecting an effort to align with those in power. Ribeiro drew a parallel to the Ishrat Jahan case, where the CBI implicated Intelligence Bureau officers, noting a similar tendency of agencies bowing to political interests.

He had, peculiarly, begun his article by mentioning my father's caste—a detail Pappa himself never really discussed. Perhaps it was to pre-empt right-wing criticism. Ribeiro also

---

[63]Ribeiro, Julio, 'Malegaon blasts case shows that Hindutva forces are succeeding in widening Hindu-Muslim divide, writes Julio Ribeiro', *indianexpress.com*, 18 May 2016, https://tinyurl.com/59xuxbx2. Accessed on 16 December 2024.

added that since my mother was dead and my sisters lived abroad, there was no one left to speak up. Since I had never given an interview, I had thankfully stopped existing.

Some of the officers who had worked with my father during the case also spoke up in an article[64] in *The Times of India*. They said they didn't want to comment on an investigation conducted by another agency, but if what they said in the chargesheet was true, 'Why have they not given a clean chit to Lt Col. Purohit?'

They further insisted it was 'not fair to suspect Karkare's investigation' because they had worked hard to present evidence in court and that they 'trusted' my father's work.

'On social media,' began an article in *Scroll*, 'supporters of a particular narrative are ecstatic at the National Investigation Agency's latest position on the 2008 Malegaon blasts case, that there is no proof against the accused.'

Saikat Dutta, the author, went on to highlight my father's bravery during the 26/11 case. He wrote that my father had rushed to Cama Hospital to aid an injured colleague with nothing but a rudimentary bulletproof jacket, designed only to withstand 9mm bullets—and a service pistol. 'Despite the lack of equipment, training, or even manpower, none of the men had hesitated to rush to help a grievously injured colleague. Why would such a man fudge an investigation to please the ruling dispensation?'

He also quoted former RAW officer A.S. Dulat, describing how my father, then Intelligence Commissioner in Mumbai, had unearthed crucial information about the man who helped fund and execute the hijacking of Indian Airlines flight IC 814 from Kathmandu, Nepal.

I didn't know what to feel except helplessness as these stories circulated on social media, in print, and on television. The lead

---

[64]Hafeez, Mateen/*TNN*, 'Karkare's officers raise doubts on NIA claims', *timesofindia.indiatimes.com*, 14 May 2016, https://tinyurl.com/4rbxs5jy. Accessed on 16 December 2024.

image for the *Scroll* article was a bird's-eye view of my father's body, draped in the national flag. Back then, I had spent a month assembling cover images for news articles. You always chose the one that stood out, the one that grabbed attention on social media. But suddenly, it felt like the most vulgar way to depict my father. Countless outlets had done it before, but now that a platform I worked for and believed in was doing the same. I felt overwhelmed with frustration.

Should I quit? I wondered to myself. *But then what else would I believe in?*

This attempt by the BJP-led government was part of a larger campaign, underway since they came to power, to dismantle the Malegaon blast investigation my father had led.

In 2021, noted journalist Josy Joseph revealed in *The Silent Coup: A History of India's Deep State*:

> Over the years, I have been told by several credible sources, in both intelligence and investigation agencies, that they suspect that Abhinav Bharat was propped up by a section of the Indian security establishment, with political blessings, to send a warning to Muslim terror groups. One former chief of an intelligence agency, who had examined the group's activities, said the idea was born sometime in 2003, and was, almost certainly, a creation of one of the intelligence agencies. Importantly, he also believed that the strategy was prompted by a foreign nation with which the then government had a well-publicized affinity.[65]

Adding that:

> Many officials also noticed that there was effort by a section in the security establishment to discourage investigations into the Hindutva terror angle, despite specific leads being available. A veteran CBI officer told me that they had

---

[65]Joseph, Josy, *op. cit.*, p. 88.

> submitted a demand to the CBI chief to question three very high-profile Hindutva ideologues, senior RSS leader Indresh Kumar, a south India-based eminent person and a retired official, but they were shut out.

Joseph concluded, 'The BJP's irrational agitation over Karkare's exposé was prompted by the fact that it was not good PR for the Hindutva family. Hindu terror is, however, a reality. Many political movements around the world mainstream themselves by shedding their violent fringes, but the BJP and its larger ecosystem have failed to do that.'

~

I didn't know if there was any other option for my sanity except to separate 'Pappa' and 'Mummy' from '26/11 Martyr Hemant Karkare' and 'Widow Kavita Karkare'. Thinking of them only through the lens of their public personas always filled me with sorrow. I thought of how Pappa had wanted to write a memoir of his own. How he had dreamed of backpacking across Europe after retirement. How his work had consumed him, often at the expense of his family. And how, after his death, government and political figures, aided by journalists who reported allegations as fact, spent years undoing the work he had done.

My mother, meanwhile, had been permanently frozen in time as a widow. Even though I was grateful to Julio Ribero for defending my father, he wrote that my mother died because 'the pain had been too much for her to endure.' But that's not how brain haemorrhages work, especially when there's hypertension and a family history.

In *Six Minutes of Terror: The Untold Story of the 7/11 Mumbai Train Blasts*,[66] she was described thus at my father's funeral:

---

[66]Sayed, N., and S. Hakim, *Six Minutes of Terror: The Untold Story of the 7/11 Mumbai Train Blasts* (Kindle ed., location 1862 of 30640), Penguin Random House India, Gurgaon, 2016.

'Everyone broke down, except his wife, Kavita Karkare. Her calm and composed face concealed the storm raging inside her. She wanted to scream and cry loudly, but chose not to. She stood silently as Aakash, their son, carried out the last rites. Her husband was a martyr and you don't cry for a martyr's death, she thought. Instead, she stared at her husband's corpse until the fire engulfed his body.'

How did they know my mother wanted to 'scream and cry loudly?' That she thought, 'you don't cry for a martyr's death?'

'I'm not a feminist and all,' my mother had once joked after reading an article about how she hadn't cried at my father's funeral, how she had done what widows were not supposed to do: combed her hair and refused to wear all white.

Does anyone really know anyone else? Aren't we all fundamentally unknowable to one another? What do you do when others begin to narrativize your parents, and you know they are wrong, but you don't know enough to correct them? You fight, sometimes violently, against letting someone else create their image inside your own head.

'Karkare's widow Kavita would devote the remaining years of her life—she died a few years later from a brain haemorrhage—to uncovering the mediocrity and malpractice that had killed her husband,' the journalist Barkha Dutt wrote in her memoir, *The Unquiet Land: Stories from India's Fault Lines*.[67]

Once someone is a widow, society insists on casting them forever as a tragic figure. But what if Mummy wasn't like that? What if, at fifty-eight, she was finally learning to let the past go? She had reconnected with old school friends, gone on vacations to the Maldives and Sri Lanka, taken up swimming and walks at Shivaji Park. She loved food and movies and was finding her way back to those interests. She died because that's what happens in life: you die, often suddenly. But while we are alive, we are living,

[67]Dutt, Barkha, *op. cit.*, p. 87.

breathing, not permanently tethered to past sorrows.

She had even begun joking, much to my awkwardness and amusement, 'Now I am going to get a boyfriend.'

Would Indian society have allowed for that outcome? Can a widow ever stop being a widow?

My father was more than a martyr; my mother, more than a widow who had fought for the truth. They were more than an officer and a teacher. They were more than just parents. They were individuals, man and woman, each embracing the complex entirety of what it means to be human. They existed beyond their professions, in their own private spaces, in the silence between thoughts.

Pappa was a difficult father. Aloof and distant. Angry often. Sometimes belittling. But Hemant was a man of many interests, widely read, and was the light of parties. One of his friends once told me they would ride their bikes, singing 'Yeh Dosti' from *Sholay* while dressed in bell-bottom pants. Another time, his closest friend recalled, 'Once we met after a long time and Hemant could not stop talking. We drove all night from Marine Drive and back.' Every so often, his carefully curated mask would slip, and at parties he would begin humming 'Kabhi Kabhie', a song S once told me had been my parents' favourite.

But 26/11 Martyr Hemant Karkare had long been claimed by others, used and repurposed for their own nefarious ends.

Kavita Karkare, however, stood apart. She was a brave woman who fought the Indian government, demanding better compensation for the families of martyrs and exposing the security lapses in the 26/11 case. She managed all this while carrying the weight of her own grief and sorrow. She had even written a poem that startled me with its raw cynicism and anger, echoing the very emotions I had harboured for years:

Do not make the mistake of becoming a martyr in this country,
as you will be branded a headless chicken

and a dumb ass who went forward (to face the threat).
'Why do martyrs get the Ashoka Chakra?'
Such will be the sophistries after your death.
The Ram Pradhan Committee will hang even the martyrs,
hence don't make the mistake of becoming a martyr in this country.
'Why was timely help not provided during 26/11
or why were the bodies lying on the road for forty minutes?'
Do not raise such questions as the wife of a martyr in this country.
But first, do not commit the crime of becoming a martyr in this country.
No country subjects their martyrs to an alcohol test. Our country does.
Do not try to understand the politics behind this.
'Why did a certain officer switch off his cell phone?'
'Or why was some officer sitting on the terrace?'
Do not stand up bravely and point fingers their way.
The compensation for martyrs got talked about a hundred times,
and the accounts of leave encashment and Provident Fund were given.
If that was not enough, there were reminders of the 15,000 rupees that were given for the last rites.
Do not make the mistake of becoming a martyr while being in a government job.
Murders are forgiven in this country.
Those who have been released from prison after being charged with corruption
can mingle amongst the masses with their heads held high.
But when you become a martyr, you become a pariah.
Do not ever commit the crime of becoming a martyr in this country.
'Should martyrs be hanged?'

'Or should their martyrdom be kept alive?'
You will decide. You will be keeping a flame that torch that we have lit.

Mummy was like us all, complicated. She loved to swim, loved food, and loved to cook. She was a wonderful mother until I was ten; after that, like most Indian parents, she would not take kindly to her children going against her plan. Yet she instilled in all of us a love for books, reading, and art. After watching the latest Hindi film, we would spend hours dissecting character motivations. *Mitra*, a movie about a couple falling in love over instant messaging, was one of her favourites. One of the most brutal films I ever watched in my childhood was with her—Mahesh Bhatt's *Zakhm*. Its themes, religion, politics, death, and grief, still echo my own story.

Mummy's maiden name was Jyotsna Deo. Jyotsna was a poet, a painter, someone who once dreamed of becoming an actor and a radio announcer.

In the aftermath of her death, I began to feel that a great violence had been committed against our family, the kind of violence we all commit on figures who suddenly become public. We strip away their humanity and reduce the real person to a headline.

My job also gave me a peek behind the curtain. I saw the pre-written obituaries prepared for celebrities who had merely been hospitalized. I overheard the newsroom discussions. 'Do we really have to do a story about 26/11 this year?' someone asked in a bored, frustrated voice when I was in office.

In that moment, all my doubts were confirmed. Now, whenever a journalist calls, I imagine the conversations behind their coverage. My father's death is a peg. No one really wants to write about it, but it might get clicks. The actual people involved don't matter. Why would they? Who really cares when they skim the news?

Oh interesting, a policeman died today. Oh interesting, the government dismantled his investigation today. Oh interesting, his wife died today. And then, flushing the toilet and moving on with their day.

Everywhere I went in the city, the city shouted back at me: *Don't forget your parents are dead.*

I decided that I would claim Mummy and Pappa for myself. When I think of them, it's the ordinary, everyday moments that surface.

My father coming home late, slipping into his light blue pajamas and vest, indulging in his favourite junk food, the one vice he allowed himself after a youth marked by scarcity. We sit together, watching TV in comfortable silence.

My mother arriving home: the doorbell rings, she steps inside, kicks off her sandals, and asks her daily question, *'Konacha fon bin?'*

They are profoundly ordinary. No one has heard of them.

Part IV

Inheritance
(2016–18)

'Orphans usually suffer from low immunity, psychiatrically speaking. You may consider getting a pet to build up your relational skills.'

—Ottessa Moshfegh, *My Year of Rest and Relaxation*

1

A hundred tiny ants

October 2016

Six months later, life, given the circumstances, was quite good. I was writing a minimum of a thousand words a day, churning out film reviews and feature articles alongside two to three articles. K and I were in a good place. I was finally getting the hang of running a household by myself. I was enjoying the freedoms that life offered a twenty-five-year-old living by themselves in a city like Mumbai. K and I could spend the day together, and I could, amongst other things, smoke and drink as I pleased.

To my friends, I even appeared privileged. A few wished—sometimes directly, other times indirectly—that their parents had died too, so that they could lead the lives they wanted. Date who they pleased, pursue the careers they dreamed of, and escape the toxicity of Indian parents who were both unwilling and unable to sever the umbilical cord binding them to their children into adulthood.

My sleep was as good as it could get. Whenever I had any trouble, I blamed my diet or the long hours I spent binge-watching the latest hit TV show or movie. Since one of my beats as a journalist was pop culture, most of this I could neatly categorize as 'work'.

For the first time, I could see myself doing an office job for four or five years, learning a few skills, making a few contacts, and then stepping out on my own as an independent artist. Music sounded good again, books filled me up with wonder and delight, and I had fallen back in love with movies. K and I even began discussing marriage.

'You're too young for that,' her dad said when she discussed it at home. That was when we realized we were getting a little carried away. We were too young.

One hot October night, I was doing what I normally did past midnight hours: watching a Netflix show with my laptop resting on my belly, lying on my custom-made seven-foot-long bed. Most of the lights were switched off except for the wooden lamp in the corner, one my father had made years ago in Chandrapur.

That was when I noticed a tingling in my extremities, the tips of my toes and fingers. It felt like the sensation of a limb falling asleep after sitting cross-legged too long. I ignored it and kept watching.

It must have been 3 or 4 a.m., that rare hour when even Mumbai seems to rest. The only signs of life in Hindu Colony were the bats from nearby Five Gardens, their wings illuminated in the yellow glow of the streetlamps as they flew through the night sky.

I rubbed my hands and feet, but the tingling continued. It seemed odd.

On one side of me lay my iPad, open to a half-read copy of Paul Kalanithi's *When Breath Becomes Air*, a memoir about the author's death from lung cancer. On the bedside table was Siddhartha Mukherjee's bestselling biography of the disease, *The Emperor of All Maladies*, with a local train ticket sticking out from the top. I wasn't reading these books solely because they were critically acclaimed works of non-fiction, but because I wanted to better understand death, and dying. I had only recently finished Atul Gawande's *Being Mortal,* which thrilled me with its frank depiction of death as a bodily function, a view I had long subscribed to even though everyone around always spoke about it in whispers.

Didn't all those books feature characters whose seemingly harmless symptoms, a persistent cough, unshakable fatigue, eventually turned out to be cancer under medical investigation?

What a stupid thought, I told myself, laughing. Still, I couldn't resist taking a step I shouldn't have. I pressed CTRL+T, opened a new tab in Google Chrome, and typed: *tingling at tips of fingers and toes.*

Out of curiosity, I clicked on WebMD. 'Diabetes', 'Peripheral Neuropathy', 'Multiple Sclerosis', 'Pernicious Anaemia', and, of course, 'Lung Cancer or Leukaemia' came up. By the time I reached that most dreaded of diseases, my heart rate had spiked. I quickly closed the tab and switched back to my Netflix show. Like most people with an internet connection, I had had my fair share of brushes with WebMD. Usually, ignoring thoughts of cancer or diabetes for a few minutes would calm me down enough to fall asleep.

But this time it didn't.

Here, I made another mistake: I went back to WebMD and kept scrolling down screen. I thought more information would help, reassure me that I was being stupid. But the word 'cancer' kept reappearing, and my heartrate refused to slow down. I finally decided to take a shower to clear my head.

Focus on diabetes, I told myself. *I could have that.* My diet wasn't particularly nutritious. Food delivery apps had just begun to take off the previous year, and as a result, I'd put on considerable weight. I didn't smoke much, just a few cigarettes at work, but that wasn't good either. Besides, both my parents had diabetes, as did two of my grandparents and one of my uncles.

I returned to bed, but cancer was all I could think about. I couldn't sleep that night. Not even at 5 a.m., when I normally did on nights like those. By morning, I felt somewhat calmer. I quickly finished my work for the day and tried to sleep by noon, but couldn't. I lay idly in bed, utterly exhausted yet completely unable to fall asleep. By evening, I decided to go for a long walk to tire myself out. After close to thirty hours without sleep, I almost looked forward to the rest I would finally get that night. I planned to walk till Sion, about three or four kilometres from my house, and then return home. Midway through my walk, my mind began to play tricks on me.

What were those unexplained bruises on my arm? I had gone to pee at least three times the night before and maybe five more times during the day. Surely that was not normal, surely it indicated something horrible. I had been breathless climbing the stairs home, more than usual. There was even a pain in my chest, at the left corner just below the ribs. Weren't these ordinary symptoms anyone could feel from time to time? But maybe, just maybe, they meant something more sinister. And the best time to act was NOW.

I ran home. Took another shower. This one didn't calm me down at all. Diabetes meant a slow, creeping death. Cancer meant a slow, painful death.

That night went the same way as the first: stand-up comedy on YouTube, relaxing sitcoms on Netflix in one tab, and articles about survival rates and cancer symptoms in another. Putting the laptop away forced me to confront these thoughts head-on, and I couldn't sit still.

After fifty hours without sleep, I decided to tell K. She didn't know how to respond. I told her not to worry, I'd sleep that night. She gave me the number of her friend, a doctor. Owing to a bizarre misunderstanding, this friend had saved my number as the mother of another acquaintance. Based on my frequent urination, my age (fifty+, female), and the burning in my feet, she suggested I might have diabetes. Now that a doctor had 'confirmed' it, I felt free to continue spiralling down the rabbit hole.

When I discovered the case of mistaken identity the following morning, the misadventures of the night before, and the one before that, took on a humorous quality. Maybe it was a sign from the universe that I did not, in fact, have diabetes. I decided to go to the office to work. I'd read somewhere that working from home could make you agoraphobic. Maybe that was what was causing my problems.

I loved the flexible hours, the freedom to set my own schedule, and the lack of commute. My height made most office spaces unbearable on a daily basis. No chair ever fit me properly, no desk gave me enough legroom, and nothing was at a comfortable eye level. Besides, the modern office environment had never appealed to me: the recycled air always gave me headaches, I loathed small talk, and with colleagues and bosses hovering around, I felt under constant surveillance, conditions I never found conducive to writing. But staying home and writing meant spending too much time inside my own head. And that was becoming an increasingly untrustworthy place.

That day, there was a birthday party at work. Cake and pizza were being passed around. I was hungry, having skipped breakfast, so I reached for a piece, then quickly pulled back.

'What's wrong with you?' I berated myself. 'You might have diabetes, you can't have sugar for lunch!'

'White sugar and white flour are two of the world's worst inventions,' Pappa would often say.

I took a piece anyway, to defy myself. I didn't want to believe I had diabetes. I was a normal adult human, and I could eat what I wanted. It was Me vs Me.

All through the workday, every time I went up and down the narrow stairs, I monitored my breathing to see if I was more breathless than before. I counted every trip to the bathroom. Checked for burning while urinating. Wondered if I was hungrier than usual. Thirstier than usual. Whenever I thought I felt a symptom, I couldn't tell whether it was new or whether I'd simply never noticed it before.

These thoughts didn't impede my writing or my conversations with any of my colleagues. I could compartmentalize my mind quite well that way. The running thread of my health however hummed in the background like a flying mosquito. I felt trapped between the devil and the deep blue sea. If testing my blood sugar confirmed my fear, my life was over. If the results came back normal, it would mean I had crossed into the world of the insane.

That night, I longed for a good sleep. I had walked all the way from Bandra to Dadar to tire myself out. I took a long, hot shower, left my laptop in the living room, and took ten deep breaths before getting into bed. I picked up a book of *Calvin and Hobbes* comics from the bookshelf and tried to read, but I couldn't concentrate. The panels blurred before me. My mind refused to quieten down.

Was I never going to be able to sleep? Would nothing convince me that I wasn't dying?

Perhaps a blood test would.

2

A complete blood count

After two mornings of dilly-dallying outside the gate of the pathology lab near my home, and two more nights of spiralling insomnia, I jumped out of bed at 8 a.m. with purpose. Before my mind could stop me, I raced up the stairs of the apartment building where the lab was located, just a few metres from my home.

'I want to do a full body check-up,' I told the receptionist, who was also a nurse.

'Which doctor has sent you?' she asked, looking up from the newspaper.

'I want to do it for myself. I have turned twenty-five, and I thought it would be a good idea.'

She raised her eyebrows for a moment, and then asked, 'Which tests do you want to do?'

Was there a correct answer? If I picked the wrong one, would she send me away?

'All of them.'

'So, WBC, CBC, blood sugar, lipid profile, liver, kidney function?'

That sounded lovely. 'Yes, all of them.'

I was sent into a room past a narrow doorway where a group of old men and women were all getting their blood drawn and handing over cups of yellow liquid. I took a seat, gave three vials of blood, and peed in a tiny jar.

I was suddenly worried. What if my tests got exchanged with theirs, and I ended up with whatever diseases they had, only to discover later, after two rounds of chemotherapy, that I didn't have cancer at all?

I ignored myself and handed over my body fluids.

I took the day off from work that day because I couldn't think of anything else but diabetes and what the results of my tests would be. If that unexplained bruise was not diabetes, maybe it was leukaemia. If my WBC count was normal, it would rule out cancer. By opting for every test on the list, I thought I'd covered all the bases.

I spent the rest of the day, reluctantly, at K's home. I hated relying on anyone this much, but her family was slowly becoming like my own. Her mother, who loved to cook, just like mine, often invited me for lunch or dinner. I used to refuse, thinking it meant intruding on someone else's family, but over time, I'd grown more comfortable. Still, telling anyone I thought I was dying of cancer felt like a bridge too far. Now was supposed to be the time for K and me to make films, take a trip to Goa, get drunk, go dancing, not sit around debating whether or not I had diabetes.

'What if it turns out I have diabetes?' I whispered to K in the living room while petting her Siamese cat, Cookie.

'You don't have it, Aakash,' she said. 'You're young.'

'But my parents had it. And you know how, in newspapers, when people experience one death, more deaths seem to follow?'

'Do you really believe that? That sounds like *vastu*.'

'But I can't help thinking my life is unlucky. All this death. It meant I never made friends in college. I studied law just to run away. And now that I'm finally picking up the pieces of my life and moving on, something else is bound to happen, I'm sure of it. This is the kind of story a novelist could turn into a critically acclaimed book.'

K laughed, and I laughed with her. For a moment, I felt calmer.

'You don't have diabetes, Aakash,' K's mother chimed in from the kitchen. I turned red. I hadn't wanted anyone else to know what I was going through. 'Even a mosquito wound doesn't heal when you have diabetes,' she added.

I glanced down at the small cut on my finger from a kitchen knife, which had lingered for days. I almost wished a mosquito would appear so I could test her theory.

By 5 p.m., my reports arrived. Blood sugar: normal. WBC and CBC: normal. But there was a high level of uric acid in my urine, my liver function was slightly off, and my cholesterol was high. My anxiety eased considerably. I didn't have diabetes!

In fact, I told myself, the anxiety had helped. If I hadn't got the tests done, the cholesterol might have clogged my arteries, and I could have dropped dead from a heart attack.

But I wasn't completely in the clear. If I wanted to sleep peacefully, I needed to find a GP that very night.

3

The first GP

Since both Dadar and Hindu Colony had large ageing populations, the area was dotted with doctors' clinics. The GP's office was a short walk from the pathology lab, and I managed to get an appointment for that very evening.

I sat with K in the waiting room for an hour before I was called in to see the doctor.

'Who's the patient?' the doctor asked, glancing at the two of us.

'I am,' I said.

'What's the problem?' he asked gruffly.

'I did these tests. I wanted you to explain them to me.'

He took the papers and went through them. 'Why did you do these tests?'

'I turned twenty-five, and I thought I should do these tests once a year. I read somewhere that you should do a health check-up every year to be safe.'

He relaxed.

'You're too young for that,' he said, smiling

He looked through the tests again. 'Cholesterol is high.'

'When did you do the test?'

'This morning at 8 o'clock.'

'When did you have dinner last night?'

'At 1 a.m.'

The stir-fried prawns I had eaten the night before felt uncomfortable in my belly.

'Then of course the results look like this,' he said. 'You need to have at least a twelve-hour gap between your last meal and the test. Do these again in three months and come back to me. In the meantime, eat healthy and exercise.'

'Thank you, doctor,' I said, and left.

K and I burst out laughing as soon as we stepped outside. We headed to our favourite neighbourhood bar, New Punjab, and ordered our usuals: a large bottle of Kingfisher Ultra, Tandoori Chicken for me, and Gobi Manchurian for her.

The doctor's words left me with no counterargument, and for once, my mind was quiet. That night, after a long hot shower, I closed my eyes and instantly fell asleep.

At 5 a.m., I woke up in a sweat.

Didn't high cholesterol lead to heart problems?

4

Another GP

I decided I needed a true professional. Not a doctor who took appointments in an ageing neighbourhood as charity for its residents after spending his day practising in private hospitals. Practo, an app that aggregated doctors, had recently been launched.

I logged on, made an account, and found a GP in Dadar West with a five-star rating. She was a woman in her thirties, with curly hair like my mother's, and degrees from a university in the US. If she thought there was nothing wrong with me, I would finally be in the clear.

I felt ridiculous sitting in the waiting room. If I told her I hadn't slept for days and was convinced I had cancer, would she call men in white uniforms to cart me off to a mental asylum? At the same time, the waiting room gave me an odd sense of calm. From now until I saw the doctor, nothing could harm me. Despite the app's assurance that appointments were guaranteed, I was eventually called in after waiting two hours.

'What seems to be the problem?' she asked me.

'Can you explain these reports?'

'Your cholesterol is high. What's your diet like?'

'I eat out mostly. Not good.'

'What about exercise?'

'I go on long walks.'

'That's not enough for a boy your age. You should go to the gym. Do these tests in three months, after these lifestyle changes, and then see me again.'

I wasn't about to spend another ₹1,500 just to be sent back to my private hell with no resolution.

'There's tingling in my extremities. I haven't slept for five days. I think I have cancer. I don't know what to do.' I said in one breath.

The doctor softened. 'Let me take your blood pressure.'

It was 160/110.

'Oh my! That is quite high. You could have high blood pressure. You should get it tested often, buy a machine, check three times a day, and report the readings to me. Have a family member help you.'

'I live alone. Is there a nurse who can come home to do it?'

'Where is your family?'

'My parents are dead.'

'How did that happen?'

'My mother died of a brain aneurysm. And my father was a police officer who was killed during the terrorist attack in Mumbai.'

She checked my name on her sheet. 'Karkare…so you are his son. Didn't your sister get married recently?'

'No, she got married long ago.'

'Oh. There was something in the papers. Weren't you in Pune?'

'No.'

She was making small talk while I was dying on the inside. She had given me another problem instead of solving the one I had. I knew that the high blood pressure was because I hadn't slept for close to a week. But if that were the case, surely she would have said something. Instead, I was convinced I was going to drop dead, just like Mummy.

'Don't worry. You will be fine,' she said at last, changing tone.

'Take Restyl,' she said, handing me a packet.

I looked at the packet of tablets and hesitantly picked it up.

'You'll feel better. Come back to me after a month.'

I took the medication when I got home, but nothing changed.

What if I got addicted? What if I ended up homeless under a bridge, desperate for my next fix?

Another sleepless night followed.

The next morning, before work, I had a moment of clarity. I realized I hadn't told the GP everything. I should have been more honest, laid out all my concerns. But where was I to find such a person, a mythical doctor who was professional, punctual, kind, and understanding? Someone who would show me the light and lift me from this anxiety, carrying me into the mythical heaven of the healthy.

If my mother were still around, I would have had access to the vast network of doctors—family friends, distant cousins, far-off uncles—she had collected over the years. She would have been invested in my health and helped me through this situation. But those phone numbers and contacts, the kind that could have offered some reassurance, went with her to the grave. Hindus don't really have graves, I suppose, so maybe 'gone up in smoke' is the more accurate phrase.

But then again, would I even have told her about my anxiety? Would I even have had this anxiety if she had never died?

It's a tricky thing, finding a good doctor when you have no reference point. With India's demographic shifts, one of the youngest populations in the world, most of the GPs who treated people when we were growing up seem to have disappeared. Or died. And new ones haven't really replaced them, because there's no money in being a general practitioner. Jack of all trades and master of none, as they say. Super-specialization is where the money is.

Online reviews aren't much help either. They're already unreliable when deciding where to order dinner from or which kitchen knife to buy. They're no better when it comes to choosing a doctor.

5

Yet another GP

The following morning, I decided to visit a GP in Matunga. I'd first accompanied one of my school friends to see the kindly old gentleman because my friend thought he was prematurely balding at fifteen. I went to Facebook to check if my friend, who I hadn't spoken to since school, still had his hair, and he did. That felt like a good enough reason to trust this doctor.

At the clinic, the receptionist handed out tokens. Each patient picked one and waited their turn in the reception area. I scanned the patients around me. A man in orthopaedic shoes caught my eye. I immediately thought it was a sign, I must have diabetes too, and one day I'd be in orthopaedic shoes. I wondered if any cancer patients were there. A long time passed in such thoughts. My number still wasn't called. Maybe I hadn't heard it while scanning for signs of dying patients, or maybe the doctor had forgotten. Just my luck: I was dying of cancer and stuck in a bureaucracy.

I didn't know what to do. I was racing against time. After this test, I had to get to work and then survive another restless night. The clock read 12.30 p.m. In half an hour, the dispensary would shut for the day. When the receptionist called a number and no one came forward; I took my chance.

Inside, I didn't bring up cancer. I only mentioned an actual symptom: the tingling at the ends of my extremities. The GP did the usual checks, looked at my tongue, examined my ears, eyes, and reflexes. Meanwhile, my mind raced, listing out every possible thing he could find. Lung cancer patients, I remembered, had clubbing at their fingertips. Their tongues showed signs too. Then he asked me to turn around, take off my t-shirt, and pressed and poked along my back. When it hurt, panic shot through me. Oh no, I thought. There's a tumour on my spine. Why else would it hurt?

'You're severely deficient in Vitamin D and B12,' the doctor finally said. We'll run a test to confirm, but you'll need a course of supplements. All Indians are deficient in Vitamin D; we don't get enough morning sunlight. Every winter, you should take a supplement course.'

Relief flooded through me. It was just vitamin deficiency. For the first time in a week, I felt relaxed, as though the constant edge I'd been living on had softened. I thought I could finally sleep when I got home. But as soon as I lay down, my head sinking into the pillow, a thought broke through: what if he hadn't diagnosed me correctly? The internet was full of stories about people who didn't know they had cancer until suddenly they dropped dead after being misdiagnosed. The anxiety returned, sharp and relentless.

Small things began to set me off. Walking down the street and spotting a life insurance ad at a bus stop felt like the universe foreshadowing my death. Flipping through the newspaper and seeing a story about cancer would send me spiralling. The Google algorithm must have thought I was a cancer researcher, because everywhere, YouTube, Facebook, Twitter, videos and articles about cancer flooded my feeds. And like a fool, I clicked. Every symptom I read about, I felt I had. The tingling stopped after a week of supplements, but now there were unexplained aches and pains all over my body.

I began checking survival rates for different cancers. Lung cancer looked grim. I Googled celebrities who had battled the disease. Lance Armstrong was cured, but testicular cancer wasn't the same as lung. Michael Douglas fought his, but that was tongue cancer. Yuvraj Singh, the Indian cricketer, had even returned to playing after his battle, but his was a tumour next to the lungs, not in them. And besides, he was an athlete.

I was an overweight twenty-something with high cholesterol who was having trouble breathing.

6

An eye test for variety

Almost two weeks had passed since my ordeal began, and my mind was slowly slipping completely out of my grasp. Deep down, I knew I didn't have cancer. I knew that I didn't have diabetes. I rarely fell sick. I could walk for ten kilometres without a break, from one end of Marine Drive and back, without getting tired.

At night, though, I felt like my vision blurred, so I went to an ophthalmologist for a checkup. He told me my eyesight was fine, though I might need a different kind of lens for my glasses. Since most doctors only accepted cash, and Modi had announced the demonetization of high-denomination currency notes, leaving ATMs empty and cash in short supply, my reserves were running dry.

With my last 5,000 rupees I decided to visit a dermatologist in Dadar West to check whether the bruises I kept noticing were of any consequence. I'd always bruised easily and I was aware of that. But still, what if?

In India, doctors almost never accept card payment. I suppose the logic is that if you are serving mankind, you can afford to scrimp on your taxes. I barely had enough left for this one more appointment.

With her, too, I felt comfortable enough to tell my entire story. She prescribed medication for the bruises, which cost 5,000 rupees, and handed me something called Bach flower remedies for my anxiety, which was essentially glorified nectar. Normally, that sort of alternative medicine would be enough to make me mistrust a doctor, but at this point, I was willing to do whatever it took. As I was leaving, she told me she had treated my mother as well. She said my mother had been a good woman, that I had nothing to worry about, and that I didn't have cancer.

I remembered then that my mother had been a hypochondriac too. It had been the cause of many fights between my parents, the large sums she spent on pills and tests, her constant self-diagnoses. To be fair, she did suffer from hyperthyroidism and hypertension, and brain aneurysms ran in the family. Maybe now was the time to bring other people into my misery. Maybe if I shared what I was going through, I would recognize the foolishness of my thinking. I confided in a friend, who revealed that she, too, was a hypochondriac.

She recommended her family doctor, someone her group of friends referred to as 'God.'

7

A GP named 'God'

When I went to meet God, I immediately saw why he was called that. He spoke calmly, asked questions that covered everything, never brushed aside my doubts or fears, and investigated each one carefully, making notes in very neat handwriting. For the first time, I felt comfortable admitting that I thought I had cancer. I pointed to the bruises on my arm, mentioned the lumps I thought I felt in my neck, and the pain in my chest. Could it be leukaemia, lymphoma, or lung cancer? The doctor smiled. Somehow, that calmed me. I could even see the humour in what I was saying, I suppose. He spoke a while longer and examined my symptoms.

He asked me to lie down flat on the bed in his room and instructed me to take deep breaths. Then he took my blood pressure, perfectly fine, already a relief compared to the other GP who had convinced me I had hypertension. I asked him again: leukaemia, pointing to the bruises; lung cancer, because of the chest pain; lymphoma, because my throat felt tight. He checked them all. He was kind, thoughtful, and even cracked a joke about my height since we were both over 6-feet tall. While he examined me, a grocery delivery arrived. He was so human, so much like me, exactly the kind of parent I had been searching for in all my encounters with doctors.

'You have nothing to fear,' he said.

'But I want to be sure,' I said. 'Is there a test I can do to know that I am completely okay?'

'No such test exists,' he replied.

'What about a full-body CT scan? I want to be sure.'

'That's too expensive. And it would expose you to harmful radiation, which actually increases your cancer risk. You wouldn't want that, would you?' he said, cracking a smile.

'I guess not,' I conceded. 'But I need to be sure. I haven't slept for a week. What can be the solution?'

'You need to trust me. You're okay. If you had cancer, it would feel different, you would know. But if a chest X-ray makes you feel better, go ahead. I can recommend India's best chest physician; he practises nearby. But I'm telling you, you are fine. What you might need is therapy.'

Since I didn't have enough cash on me, he let me pay later. He prescribed statins for high cholesterol (which, yes, raise diabetes risk by five per cent, but I'd worry about that another day). I felt as though a huge weight had lifted from my shoulders. He suggested I stay with friends, but I didn't have any I could rely on to that extent. He suggested relatives, but I disliked mine enough that staying with them would've been as miserable as the anxiety itself. Living with my girlfriend and her parents wasn't an option either. I wanted to be in my own bed, in my own space, like a normal adult human being.

I felt more relaxed than I had since the ordeal began. To celebrate, I smoked a cigarette and ate pav bhaji. Then I walked from Grant Road to Dadar—ten kilometres—hoping exhaustion would finally let me sleep. And it did, for two hours. Then I woke up again, dread rushing back in. What if I still had cancer? After all, even Amartya Sen had once been misdiagnosed. He had gone to the library, found the correct diagnosis, and gone on to win the Nobel Prize. Doctors weren't God; they didn't know everything. I stayed awake until 8.30 a.m. and called him again.

I had also been reading Rana Dasgupta's *Capital*, with its chilling chapter on Delhi's private healthcare system. Trust no one, it said.

So, I went back to see God, embarrassed at wasting his time.

'I am very scared, doctor. My chest hurts, I am breathless. I really think I need to go for a full-body checkup.'

'Okay,' he said. 'Why don't you do it? We should investigate everything.'

This time, I went to a reputable clinic for a more comprehensive set of tests. I added a thyroid test to rule out thyroid or throat cancer, plus Vitamin A, B12, D, C, calcium, and iron.

'Why are you doing all these tests?' the resident doctor at the clinic asked me.

'My neck hurts,' I replied.

'Are you related to Hemant Karkare?'

'Yes. He was my father.'

'Oh, okay. We will try to help you.'

Great, I thought. All the looks of pity I'd collected over the years had finally culminated here. The famous orphan of Dadar had cracked—at least that's what they must be thinking.

Everything came back normal. For a few days, my anxiety dulled to a lower level. I even slept an hour or two at night. But over two weeks, I had barely slept ten hours.

I grew claustrophobic in my own home, terrified of the night because that's when the thoughts attacked with full intensity. At 5 a.m., I took the first chance to escape and drove to Marine Drive, the famous seaside promenade. Amongst the joggers, I felt a sliver of normalcy. They were running for health; I was walking fast to check if I was dying.

I remembered an article about a woman in her twenties who went jogging, felt a sharp pain in her chest, and convinced herself she had lung cancer. She insisted on scans and a biopsy despite being dismissed by doctors, and she was right. Stage 2 lung cancer. I jogged too, pressing hard on my chest to test for pain. Nothing. Maybe I was fine. Or maybe I wasn't exerting myself enough, wasn't testing properly. I ran faster, got a stitch in my side, and fell into the endless ouroboros of health anxiety.

I went on forums, read other people's stories. Some seemed worse off. A patient in the UK, convinced they were dying, couldn't get an appointment. Someone else thought the universe was warning them when an empty hearse passed in front of them. I laughed at the absurdity—mine, theirs. But laughter didn't convince me.

A rational side of me knew I wasn't sick. But my mind and body only obeyed the crazed side, the one convinced death was imminent. Nothing I did could silence it.

I took the stairs everywhere. I walked for hours. From Dadar to Bandra. From hospital to hospital. Testing myself: was I breathless? Exercise is supposed to help, fights anxiety, improves mood, releases endorphins. I even took up tennis again. On the surface, I was functioning. I was going to work. Paying all my bills on time. Sometimes hanging out with K and her friends, who had become my friends as well. But at the bottom of my belly, the feeling of anxiety never really left me. I hadn't considered how all of this was affecting K. One night, after I went over all my imaginary symptoms with her, she broke. 'I can't take this anymore. You need to see a psychiatrist.'

For me, that was unthinkable. My mother once suggested my father see a psychiatrist friend for his anger issues. 'That fool?' my father had scoffed. 'He's a divorcee. How can he help me if he can't even save his own family?' Werner Herzog, another of my surrogate parents, also scorned therapy, blaming it for the ills of the 20th century. I didn't believe them, not fully, but still, therapy felt like a step too far.

'Maybe we should break up,' K said.

'I don't want to. I love you.'

'I do too,' she whispered. 'But it's too much for me.'

'Okay, I'll go for therapy,' I said. 'You're my best friend. My only family. I don't want to lose you, especially not to something I can't control. I don't even know what's happening to me.'

'Okay,' she said.

That night, I dropped her home and texted an old friend—a guidance counsellor. I asked if she knew of a therapist or psychiatrist who could help me, because I could no longer sleep at all.

8

The first psychiatrist

I set up an appointment with a psychiatrist at nearby Sion Hospital, quite reluctantly. I called the doctor and hesitatingly explained my problems, that I had trouble sleeping, that I kept thinking I had cancer. He hummed and hawed before offering me a list of options for an appointment. I took the earliest one I could get.

Since Sion Hospital was government-run, I was worried. Those places weren't much good for regular illnesses; how could they possibly be any better for mental illness? What if I ended up like one of the patients from *One Flew Over the Cuckoo's Nest*? But there weren't many options. I didn't know anyone who had gone for therapy or seen a psychiatrist. So he seemed like the best, and only, choice.

I rolled out of bed at 8 a.m., after another sleepless night. The walk was only thirty minutes, but I left two hours early. Mornings felt like the only balm against anxiety. The hot rays of the sun on my neck as I walked from Dadar to Sion calmed me. I used to love the night for its quiet and stillness. I had never been a morning person; I had always been most comfortable inside my head. But now both my mind and the night had betrayed me.

I waited by the gates of Sion Hospital, unwilling to cross the barrier. Once I went in and saw a psychiatrist, it felt like I would cross an invisible line in the sand, moving from the world of the sane into the world of the insane.

What if there was no turning back? What if I discovered things about myself that were best left hidden?

I drifted aimlessly through the hospital, staring at the faces of people around me.

How many had life-threatening illnesses? How many were in situations like mine?

Unable to find the right building, I asked a staff member at a nearby reception desk for directions. He pointed me the right way, but I wondered if he'd looked at me a second too long, perhaps thinking, *so this is what crazy looks like.*

I walked as slowly as I could up the staircase to the doctor's office, hoping to avoid spending too much time in the waiting room, where attendants might talk to me or other patients might ask why I was there. The doctor was inside with another patient. The door was open!

I could see and hear everything happening inside. The doctor was laughing, which I thought might be a good sign. But I didn't want my therapy session to become theatre for the other denizens of the hospital. I unfocused my hearing so I couldn't listen to more, even though I was curious.

Indignation rose in me. Where was the long brown couch? The understanding middle-aged man or woman with a kindly face who would listen to my problems, speaking in soft, measured tones, revealing things about myself I didn't know, answering the questions that had burned inside me for years? Movies had lied to me! Instead, I got a random man at a crowded desk, whose advice sounded like a mixture of Dale Carnegie and WhatsApp forwards. I wanted to leave, but I had come this far, and been sent by a friend. I took a deep breath and centred myself.

Stop being cynical, I told myself. *Maybe this will help. Maybe your cynicism is what got you here in the first place.*

I walked in, sat down across from the doctor, and looked at his smiling face. Sunlight poured in from the window to the left. I glanced at him, then at the door. He didn't get the hint, and only looked at me expectantly. I waited for a sign to begin, but none came. So I launched into my sorry tale. He nodded after each sentence. Voicing aloud everything that had plagued me over the past two weeks made me feel lighter. It all sounded childish and trivial, not nearly as crazy as it had inside my head. He laughed. I laughed.

This twenty-five-year-old, convinced he's dying of cancer? How absurd. How comic.

'So, you have what we call health anxiety,' he said.

'Okay,' I replied.

Ah, a proud member of the Mr Obvious community.

'What can I do about it?'

'Right now, your mind is in a very crazy state. I can start therapy, but your mind won't accept it. Do you want to take medicine?'

I hadn't slept for ten days. Why was he expecting me to make a decision? What did I know about whether medication would help? Most of what I'd read made it seem like pills led only to addiction, numbness, and never feeling normal again.

'The GP gave me this medicine,' I said.

'How many times a day are you taking it?'

'She told me to take it once.'

'You're supposed to take it three times, my friend. Otherwise, it won't work. Why don't you do that and come back in three weeks?'

I walked out feeling relieved and calm, lighter than before. A huge weight seemed to have lifted. But I couldn't tell if it would last, or if it was only temporary relief.

Was that what therapy looked like? Weren't sessions in movies supposed to end with some big breakthrough? What about a good night's sleep? He hadn't mentioned it. He hadn't said a word about the side effects of the medication.

Doctors just kept sending you away, promising to see you after three weeks. What miracle was supposed to happen in that time? Maybe it was some kind of quality-control trick taught in medical school. Perhaps all the doomed patients would die in that period, leaving doctors free to work with the resilient souls who survived.

Humankind had proved futile. So it was back to the benevolence of the algorithm on Practo. I narrowed my search. Distance and price were my top priorities, nothing over 1,000 rupees and nothing that forced me to crawl through Bombay traffic before work. And the platform had to guarantee appointments. I found a workable solution: a clinic on the way to work, with a fee of 850 rupees.

9

A better psychiatrist

The reviews weren't encouraging: *'Doctor was absent for appointment without prior notice at time of appointment. Please inform beforehand'* and *'It was my first visit. She came late and I guess she was in a hurry as quite a few patients were waiting, so I was not satisfied with the way she listened and addressed the problem. [sic]'*

Still, she had a 4.5 rating, the same metric I used for food delivery. Plus, she looked like my mother, had curly hair, and her office was near the Portuguese Church in Dadar West, where my grandmother had lived. She held both an MBBS degree and a master's in psychology from Mumbai University. She was both a therapist and a psychiatrist.

I made my way to her office through the winding corridors of a tenement building directly opposite Portuguese Church. Through the glass door, I could see a tiny bench where, much like a crowded seat on the local train, five people were crammed into a space meant for three. I waited outside. Three more men were ahead of me, all with I-cards around their necks. Perhaps there for a mandatory corporate mental health check-up.

My appointment time came and went. When I stepped inside, the receptionist instantly told me to go back out.

'But…but I have an appointment,' I said.

'We don't have appointments. We work on first-cum-first-serve basis only,' she said curtly.

So, I waited for another forty-five minutes on the balcony outside the glass door, on a hot Mumbai evening, staring at the passing traffic as rivulets of sweat trickled down my back

Eventually, the receptionist called me inside, handed me a consent form, and directed me to another room a few feet away. It wasn't the doctor's office, just *Waiting Room No. 2.* There were fewer people here. Two children sat next to their mothers, chatting with a young woman about my age who was laughing with them.

Were children also getting anxiety these days? Had the Western epidemic of ADHD visited Indian shores without my noticing?

An attendant came to collect my consent form and handed me a pencil and a blank piece of paper. I looked up at her, puzzled.

'Draw a picture of a home, family, and scenery,' she instructed.

I stared at the paper for a while then laughed to myself. I felt like a child being admitted to kindergarten. The only drawing class I had ever taken ended with the instructor announcing loudly to the class: *'I told this boy to draw a stick figure human. He has drawn what looks like a mosquito.'*

Was there a right answer? What would the therapist read into my drawing? Should I put windows on the house? If I drew the family in separate rooms, would it suggest something about my state of mind? Maybe I should mess with her and draw the perfect happy family, that would be a laugh. For whom, I didn't know.

In the end, I retreated to the familiar image Indian children are taught to draw: a hut by the mountains and a river. After I finished, I held the paper face down, lest anyone analyse my ridiculously bad drawing skills and assume I was mad. I didn't know if that was the intention, but the waiting and drawing had succeeded in calming me. For the moment, whether I had cancer or not, all I could do was wait.

I found myself in a conundrum. What little I knew about therapy suggested it only worked if the patient was honest. But how honest could I be? I was perpetually afraid that whatever I revealed about my parents might end up as gossip for a third party. What if, like the endless journalists and screenwriters reaching out to me for 'life rights', the doctor turned my confession into a bestselling book? Besides, I had come to believe it was nearly impossible for a therapist who had enjoyed a normal childhood, a happy family, and parents who had survived into old age to understand what I was going through. But there were no apps for orphans to find therapists who were orphans, so there was no point dwelling on it.

After another interminable wait, the young woman who had been chatting with the children came over to me.

'So, the doctor will not be able to see you today. She has too many appointments. But I will take your session today. I am currently doing my master's in psychology at Mumbai University and interning with ma'am.'

'Okay,' I replied.

She asked for my drawing. I handed it over. She looked at it for a second but made no comment before putting it away.

'So, tell me,' she said.

'I can't sleep,' I began.

'Okay, why?'

'Umm… I think I have cancer. At night, when I try to sleep, I cannot think of anything else. I probably know that I don't have it, but my heart rate shoots up. I can't calm myself, no matter whatever I do. It's been happening for several weeks now.'

'Okay. How old are you?'

'I'm twenty-five.'

'What do you do?'

'I'm a journalist.'

'Are you from Mumbai?'

'Yes.'

'Do you live with your parents?'

'No.'

'Where do your parents stay?'

'They are dead.'

'How?'

'My mother had a brain haemorrhage. My father was a police officer. He died in 26/11,' I said flatly, without emotion.

She raised her eyebrows but didn't ask any more questions. She treated it matter-of-factly and continued. Ah, medical professionals at least knew that such things were a common part of life.

I wasn't sure what I had hoped to get from therapy. I didn't believe in most Indian institutions. Whether because of my experiences or because I was simply a cynical person, I could no longer tell. What I wanted was some kind of catharsis. A long cry. A resolution to the mystery of my life. The perfect denouement. To heal from years of death and grief, then go home and sleep so I could continue to be a writer. That the past would fix itself, the wounds would close, and I could finally move on.

We spoke for another twenty minutes. I listed out my various symptoms, the various diseases I thought I could have.

Diabetes?

'Oh, that's quite manageable.'

High BP?

Her mother had it. Also, quite manageable.

'Why fixate on cancer? Especially after all those tests? That means it has to be in your mind,' she said.

'Yes, I know. I am aware. But I cannot function without sleeping. I can't keep thinking about all these things all the time. It has to stop.'

'Try meditating. It really helps.'

'Okay,' I said.

'How are you feeling now?'

'Relieved, I guess. I hope I can sleep tonight.'

'You will be able to. I'm sure of it.'

'Okay, thank you.'

'Come back next week. Ma'am will be available to see you then.'

I walked out feeling lighter than I ever had after visits to GPs or the psychiatrist at Sion Hospital. Perhaps this was what the talking cure meant, you had to speak about your problems again and again until they felt ordinary, until you felt lighter.

That night, I slept for a few hours, then tossed and turned for a few more. I woke up groggy, dragged myself out of bed, and went to work. By night, I was back in my spirals.

Maybe it was a failure on my part. Maybe I hadn't managed to convey the severity of what was happening to me. Maybe this was some delayed grief from when I was seventeen. Maybe we needed to probe deeper and deeper into my subconscious.

10

More adventures with the better psychiatrist

'You are feeling very relaxed,' the therapist said in a mishmash of accents, an American twang mixed with something I couldn't quite place, maybe the clipped tone of an old-school BBC anchor. 'From the tips of your fingers to the tips of your toes,' she continued in her sing-song style, mimicking the soothing cadences of mindfulness app hosts.

She sat at her desk, with her hands in a triangle fold, looking straight ahead at a fixed point on the wall in front of her. I was lying down, socks on, shoes off, in the corner of her cramped room, on a mattress, precariously positioned on a row of file cabinets, staring at the white ceiling. My feet stuck out at one end and my shoulders were hunched up against the wall. A smell of camphor hung in the air. Soft sitar music played on her phone, part of a meditation playlist, the same gentle chord, every few seconds.

'Reflect on your pain, from the tips of your toes to the tips of your fingers.'

My mind began drifting off: what was I going to cook for dinner? A bunch of coriander lay rotting in the fridge. What could I possibly use it for? I was getting sleepy. For once, I felt relaxed in this little air-conditioned room I didn't have to pay the bills for, my anxious mind soothed by the thought that at least I was trying to fix my problem.

From here, I had to rush onwards to a press screening, another superhero film from Hollywood.

'Talk to your pain,' she said suddenly, barging into my

mind's wanderings. 'Take a deep breath. Go on. Ask it why it is bothering you. Say to it, 'What do you want from me, pain?'

I took a deep breath and did as the doctor told me. No pain answered back.

I had returned to the therapist-psychiatrist in Dadar West. This time there had been no discussion with interns. I had gotten to see 'ma'am' herself, and once we finished our brief meditation, we began the session.

'So, what brings you here?' she asked me.

I wanted to sound witty, maybe even erudite. Maybe say something smart. Quote a figure. Say something clever. My only references were movies, maybe something like, 'What else? We are all mad here.' But that would be useless. So instead, I recited the usual litany: can't sleep, dead parents, fear of cancer, journalist, twenty-five years old, live alone, have a girlfriend, sisters abroad, not close to family.

'Yes...oh... Karkare...you are his son?'

'Yes.'

'That's quite traumatic.'

'I guess.'

'How long has it been this way?'

'I haven't slept at all for two weeks now. But ever since my mother died and I started living alone, I became afraid of the night. I kept thinking someone would attack me. Thieves would break in and kill me.'

'Not easy living alone, no?'

'I guess.'

'Do you miss your parents?'

'I'm not sure. We weren't really close. It's been so long. I don't remember.'

'Your dad was a great man.'

'Yes, okay.'

'Your mother, you must miss her?'

'I don't really think about all those things. I try not to.'

'Okay.'

'Do you like your job?'

'Yeah, mostly.'

'Any stress at work?'

'Not really. I just think about writing and movies all the time. I can't switch off, but I don't think I am stressed out about it.'

'What about your relationship?'

'It's fine.'

Bringing up the conversation I'd had with K about a possible break-up felt like a betrayal of her confidence. Besides, that wasn't why I was here.

'See Aakash, what you have is health anxiety. It is an extreme form, and I don't think therapy alone will work for you right now. We need you to calm down first. I will prescribe some medications which will ease things, and then we can continue.'

'Let us meet again in two weeks.'

The wave of relief that hit me was tremendous. It was as though a heavy chunk of lead lodged in my stomach had finally melted away. I had admitted to a stranger that I wasn't close to my parents, that I wasn't sure I missed them. And she had acknowledged my pain. She had told me my life had been difficult. I hadn't even realized I wanted someone to say that.

She prescribed Clonazepam for emergencies, and Mirtazapine to be taken twice daily. I immediately googled the side effects: weight gain, ejaculatory disturbance, brain fog, gastric issues, insomnia.

Why hadn't she mentioned any of this? Could she be trusted?

11

Even more adventures with the better psychiatrist

Two weeks later, I found myself in the second office with a blank piece of paper and a pencil. I drew the same picture once again. The medications had helped, but they left me groggy in the mornings. I had digestion troubles, and it felt as though there was a fog following me around. Sometimes a random incident would spike my anxiety, and I'd take a Clonazepam. As the pill melted into medicine-y sweetness under my tongue, I'd feel my heart rate calm down. Absurd incidents still occurred, like during a press screening of the animated movie, *Sing*, when I became convinced I felt tumours in my neck and had to leave halfway. I went home, downloaded a cam print off the internet, and filed my review.

Two hours later, 'Doctor Ma'am' called me in.

We had the same conversation about my symptoms. She answered all my thought spirals with logic. This time, though, she gave me a new piece of advice that was oddly calming.

'Do you have a low-grade fever?'

'What do you mean?'

'A fever of 100 degrees. If you have cancer, that's what you have all the time.'

'Not that I know of,' I said, relieved, but also making a mental note to buy a thermometer on my way home.

'So, Aakash, when you have cancer, you know. It's a different pain.'

Her words only added to the long list of questions I asked myself every day: Am I peeing too much? Are there random bruises on my arm? Is this a different pain? Do I have a low-grade fever? Is this a different pain?

Over the next couple of months, our sessions fell into a pattern. We'd talk for a while, then do a meditation exercise where I tried to speak with my pain, and finally she'd send me off with another prescription. No mention was ever made of how long this would last, or when I could return to living a life without anxiety. I didn't even ask.

Sometimes I'd see the medicine salesman stop by, offering deals on all kinds of antipsychotic drugs. I tried not to grow cynical about the mental health business.

Talking never helped as much as it had in the first few sessions. Back then, it had felt like all the grief and wounds from my parents' deaths, long wrapped in invisible bandages around my heart, had suddenly burst open in 2016, and everything I had buried came rushing out. I hadn't known what to do with it, so my mind had latched onto cancer.

But what if I actually had it? What if it was already too late?

The only thing that worked were the pills, though even those came with frustration. The wait times stretched from thirty minutes to two hours. Sometimes the doctor forgot to inform me she was on holiday, and I'd sit in traffic over Tilak Bridge, get late to work, and leave with nothing. When I ran out of pills, I'd have to rush back again, only to find her gone some days. Whether the therapy was working or not, I couldn't tell. When I couldn't refill the prescriptions, the anxiety returned in full force.

Eventually, I decided to find a more convenient doctor, someone who could at least refill the prescriptions without all the chaos. By then, I was slowly working my way back to eight hours of sleep. Already, it seemed as if I was becoming happier. Calmer. More relaxed.

12

A psychiatrist who keeps his appointments

I found another psychiatrist in Sion who charged a reasonable 800-rupee fee and whose clinic was in the opposite direction of morning rush-hour traffic from my home in Dadar. Once again, I booked the earliest appointment at 8 a.m.

When I arrived, only the receptionist was in. She phoned the doctor, who eventually rushed in half an hour later, suitcase in hand, hair dishevelled, shirt untucked. He looked irritated. It seemed he had forgotten the appointment, or perhaps that he was even listed on the app. Maybe his assistant hadn't told him, and he had had to wake up just for me.

After a few minutes, he called me in. As soon as I stepped through the door, a distinct smell hit me. Flatulence, perhaps. Was that a sign? A metaphor? I set the thought aside and recounted the usual details.

'So, you are having a lot of ruminations?' he asked.

'Yes.'

'For how long?'

'It's been a few months, but I think I've had this anxiety simmering at the back of my head for a long time. I don't know when it started. But in the evenings, I feel a creeping sense of dread. Only now has it become unmanageable.'

'So, these ruminations come at night?'

'They are there during the day too, but the intensity increases at night.'

'Hmm. Okay, I understand. So you've been having ruminations for many years. I see.'

He finished scrawling something on a piece of paper. 'Take these medicines and come back to me in three weeks.'

'How long should I take these medicines?'

'You have been ruminating for years. It will take two to three years at least.'

Alarm bells. Three years of medication? Maybe this guy was in cahoots with the pharmaceutical companies. I'd get addicted, have to keep coming back here for another fix. Still, he prescribed me two different SSRIs and Clonazepam.

That night, I finally slept.

The next morning, I woke up feeling completely refreshed, for the first time in months. I told myself I had misjudged him. He had given me the perfect cocktail of drugs.

Over the next few weeks, I felt light return to my days. The voice in my head fell silent. Was this what it felt like to be 'normal'? This was what it was like to live without your mind playing tricks on you. I could lose myself fully in the moment. Focus on work. Go out with friends. Spend time with K without the constant shadow of death lurking. I no longer ran through a never-ending list of worst-case scenarios.

13

But then unfortunately disappears into the ether

When I returned after three weeks, there was a different receptionist, and the sign board had been removed. I walked in and asked if the doctor was in. She gave me a blank look.

'Who? No one by that name practises here.'

Maybe I had the wrong floor. I checked again, but there was no sign of the man anywhere. I went downstairs and asked the security guard about the doctor who had been obsessed with ruminations.

'Oh, that guy? He just disappeared one day and went off to Gujarat. No one has seen him for three weeks,' he said, scratching his white beard.

I felt trapped in a horror film. Had I imagined him? He had seemed a little peculiar. But then who had written the prescriptions?

I began to speculate, piecing together possibilities from news reports I had read about psychiatrists. Maybe one of his patients had attempted, or even died by, suicide, a police complaint had been filed, and he had absconded. Of course, there was probably a simpler explanation. But in my state of mind, why would I put my faith in that?

14

A psychiatrist within walking distance (who also disappears)

I decided to find another psychiatrist, this time within walking distance of my home. He had fifteen years of experience, something I could at least take as a positive. The waiting room, where shoes were not allowed, carried the depressing air of a government office. Only two people were waiting. Already, that felt like a better sign. He called me in after just fifteen minutes. Hurray.

I recounted my story again, feeling like a witness at a crime scene giving testimony. By now, I had edited it down to the essentials, concise, efficient, hitting only the emotional beats. I had lost faith in talk therapy. Just give the medicine so I can go home and sleep.

He stared at me with a nod and a grin. Something about his eyes seemed shifty, untrustworthy. But what was I supposed to do?

'Do you exercise?' he asked.

'Sometimes.'

'What about diet?' he added, my answer having confirmed something to him.

'I eat out often.'

'Those are the problems,' he said with pride, having hit the nail on the head.

If only I had met the man four months ago, all my problems would have been solved.

'Yes, I know. I am trying. But I can't stop thinking about cancer long enough to try. I just want to be able to sleep.'

'Have you tried meditation?'

'Yes. But then I only think that I am going to die.'

'Okay, if you want, I will prescribe these medications. But I think you should lift weights. And meditate.'

'I have been going for therapy.'

'All of that is pointless. These are the problems created by our modern life. Exercise, eat right, meditate, pray and sleep. Everything will be solved.'

'Yes, I will. Thank you,' I said through gritted teeth, throttling the urge to ask him why he had spent four years getting an MBBS degree and then a psychiatry specialization when he could have simply become a gym trainer.

Years later, when both Virat Kohli and Michael Phelps revealed they had struggled with anxiety, I was tempted to send an email to that doctor, but I doubted he even had an email address.

Two weeks later, when I returned to fill the prescription, I discovered there was a different doctor in the office. His specialization: orthopaedics.

'What happened to the psychiatrist?' I asked the receptionist.

She looked at me, puzzled.

Oh no. Not again.

I walked out, and across the street I noticed a sign. My psychiatrist had moved to an office just five minutes away. I trailed through its endless corridors, the building stinking of urine and musty air, as if no window had been opened since it was built. Finally, I reached his new office.

'I'm here to see the doctor,' I told the receptionist.

'He is on holiday,' she replied flatly.

My face must have betrayed the panic of a man who had run out of medication on a Friday, which meant I couldn't get a refill until Monday. She asked, 'Is it an emergency?'

Normally, I would have said no. But I reached into my well of shame and said, 'Yes. I've run out of medication.'

'Oh, sorry. We can't help with that. We need his signature.'

What if I had said I was suicidal? Would they have helped then? Maybe the doctor would have suggested a kickboxing class. Who knows, maybe it would have helped.

'Okay, thanks anyway.'

I walked out, wondering why so many doctors seemed to vanish, selling offices, moving, going out of town. Maybe, because there's no official licensing body in India, these psychiatrists were actually former criminals, their pasts catching up with them. That would explain the chaos of their practices.

What if I had been some kind of psychopath who went on a murder rampage every time I ran out of medication? How could these doctors just prescribe pills and then vanish?

Resigned, I went back to the app and booked an appointment with the psychiatrist-therapist of the indeterminate accent.

15

Back to the better psychiatrist

Four or five months had passed in all these doctor visits. Sometimes I slept for eight hours, sometimes only two. Most days I was convinced I had cancer, and most days I knew I was being ridiculous for thinking so. I spent my days going for film reviews, interviewing filmmakers and musicians, trying to come up with feature articles to write.

I had begun to think I would never be free of this problem. One of my colleagues, with whom I often went for lunch followed by chai and a cigarette, once asked why I had stopped smoking.

'Oh, I'm worried about getting cancer,' I said.

He laughed, and I grinned. He didn't know I was being serious.

For years I had avoided confronting the deaths of my parents, postponing any anxiety to some future date when I thought my dreams might finally be realized. I wasn't sure if what I felt back then was anxiety, but I remembered a creeping sensation in my belly during evenings at ILS College. Had that been depression? I recalled having that sensation for most of my life. Every evening, fear would take hold when my father was due to come home. Whenever conversations drifted to my parents, or when someone asked me about '26/11 Martyr Hemant Karkare', I felt that same sinking in my stomach.

I thought this feeling would vanish once I had arrived at the life I imagined: a happy relationship, a good job, and a path toward realizing my dreams. But it was precisely then, six months ago, that this peculiar obsession with cancer took root. I could still think logically while all this was happening. Yet, there was something inside my mind that had taken on a life of its own. People had often seen me as calm, always able to withstand the most stressful situations, emotional or physical. I couldn't understand why my mind was unravelling now, when life finally seemed good.

Maybe I had never truly succeeded in escaping 26/11 and its many afterlives. In running away from it with all my might, I had been running directly toward it. The wounds were still as raw as they had been at seventeen and twenty-three. The thought of my parents' bodies consumed in smoke and turned to ash still filled me with the same unbearable pain. Time had not healed. It was one thing to know this logically, to recognize the connection between my fixation on cancer and my parents' deaths, but how to convince my mind, so that I didn't have to live with these thoughts every single day?

I had begun in December, and now it was March. Over those four months, sessions had shifted from fortnightly to monthly, from talk therapy to guided meditation. From my therapist's full, focused interest, when my case still seemed unique, to the idle, listless boredom of a school kid.

The medications no longer helped as they once had. Their best purpose now was to help me sleep. I woke up groggy, my digestion was unsettled, and there was a strange dampening of my emotions. It felt as if I were looking at my feelings through a rain-smeared car window, and only occasionally would a raindrop slide down, allowing a fleeting moment of clarity amidst all the blurring.

After yet another meandering session, I looked directly into her eyes and said with some seriousness, 'I'm not all better. It's simply not like before. Am I going to have to deal with this all my life?'

'Maybe something plagues you deep within.'

'Maybe it does but what can we do about it?'

She thought for a moment, and then grinned. It was the

grin of a magician about to bamboozle you with a trick up their sleeve. She leaned forward, wrapped the *pallu* of her saree around her, and then resumed the triangle fold on the register in front of her.

Was I about to ascend to the next level of therapy? Had my mind reached the point where I could accept it? Level 1 had been the intern and the drawing class. Level 2 was talk therapy. Level 3, guided meditation. If this were a video game, was I about to face the equivalent of a boss fight?

'Where do you see yourself in five years?'

God, this was now turning into a job interview. Maybe, since I was paying her and didn't need to worry if I was getting hired, I could respond like that stand-up comedian once joked: I should look at my watch, then look up and say, 'Well, let's see… It is lunch time now… So five years from now, I will most probably be eating lunch.'

I desisted. My anxiety had taken my humour away from me.

'I don't really know. I like my job. Hopefully, I am still doing it. Maybe I have finished a book. Maybe I am applying to a Ph.D., because that's the only way someone who's studied the humanities can leave the country. Maybe I have travelled more. But that is about it.'

The smile reduced in its intensity. I had bamboozled her somehow.

'So, you don't want a BMW?' she asked, certain she had caught me in my tracks.

'I don't think so…'

'Interesting. You don't want to be a CEO?' she asked, the smile had turned into puzzlement.

'No… I mean…of what?'

'That's what most men in your generation want. Do you know that?'

'Umm… I guess…'

I tried to recall if anyone my age had ever expressed such

desires. A few had mentioned wanting fancy cars, but no one had talked about wanting to be a CEO. I did know some people working on their start-ups, maybe that's who she meant. Perhaps it wasn't right for a twenty-five-year-old man not to want those things. Maybe it meant I lacked ambition or drive. My idols had never been people with BMWs or suit-wearing CEOs, and maybe that was the problem. If I woke up one day as a CEO with a sports car and a model wife, maybe then I wouldn't think I had cancer. Was that what she was trying to tell me? We both stared at each other for a while.

'Have you thought about prayer?'

'Thought what about it?'

'You know praying?'

'Not really, no. I don't believe in God.'

'You can still pray.'

'To whom?'

Again, no answer,

'Then do you know why this is happening?'

'I have no idea. Maybe that's what life is, you know. Shit keeps happening. I thought I was happy and then suddenly I am convinced I have cancer.'

'Let us pick up next time. I think we are close to something here.'

I got up in a strange kind of daze. I was desperately looking for the cure to what was ailing me. Perhaps, there was none. I wasn't insane I guess and maybe I should take joy in that knowledge. For the rest of my life, I would be worried about cancer. Unless it killed me shortly because it was in Stage 4. In a peculiar way, I almost wished I had it, because then at least it would be a tangible problem, something I could resolve through chemo, or surgery and get a prognosis for. With my hypochondria, it seemed like there was no cure.

I had worried about exactly this situation before I had begun my journey into this world of mental health. I had always felt that my problem was too weird for them. My experiences had marked me in some way. I was different from other people, and not in a good way. What could a therapist who hadn't experienced what I had experienced know about what ailed me? Or about the philosophical crises I wrestled with daily? I looked at life too strangely, too bizarrely. Maybe all the weird looks people over the years gave me whenever they discovered my backstory were right after all. I didn't even want a BMW, which seemed to be what everyone else my age wanted. Maybe the process of chasing that dream was so arduous that you didn't have time to think about anything else. For me, it always circled back to the same thing: I was trapped in a great philosophical crisis, the struggle to recreate meaning after everything I believed in had been shattered when Pappa and Mummy had died .

Everything was doomed. I remember thinking that as I left that session. When my father passed, I was only seventeen, and I could still tell myself that things would be okay, that better things lay ahead. Death happens in many lives. Life was long. But my mother's death had shattered that illusion. Now nothing stood between me and the great beyond. I was next in line for death, and knowing my luck, it would come when I least expected it.

After my mother died, I began calculating my age and remaining time in numbers. At twenty-three, I had thirty-one years left if I died at my father's age, and thirty-five if at my mother's. At thirty, it became twenty-four and twenty-eight. That left me with just over two decades to write the novels I wanted to write, to travel the world, and to do all the things I thought I wanted to do. At thirty-four, I will have lived as many years without a father as with one. At forty-six, I will have lived as many years as an orphan as with parents. And so on. I don't know what purpose this thinking serves, but in idle moments, especially before bed, it's easy to fall into these thoughts.

I began to have the same old nightly panics. I still researched ways to confirm, once and for all, that I was cancer-free. I found a website with a 'lifetime map' of tests, outlining what to do at every age group and the network of medical professionals one was supposed to cultivate.

One night, around 11 p.m., I was driving a friend to the airport. She was on an internship in India from Germany. Suddenly, panic hit me. I couldn't drive. I pulled over, breathless, dark bruises forming on my arm, and called the doctor people called 'God.'

'I'm convinced I have leukaemia,' I told him.

'You are fine,' he said. 'These are all symptoms of anxiety. Trust me.'

His calm voice made me feel better. I thanked him. Apologized for calling so late. I felt embarrassed. There was silence in the car.

'My grandparents and my mother all had cancer. My grandmother's case is terminal,' my friend said quietly.

'Don't you feel scared that you might inherit it?'

'What's the point in that? Whatever has to happen will happen. No point in worrying about it.'

It seemed like sound logic. But try as I might, I was unable to convince myself of it. Neither could the therapists I was paying thousands of rupees to.

16

Dr R: A new hope

'I don't know what to do anymore,' I complained to K. 'I guess this is my life from now. I never wanted this anxiety. I don't want to live with it.'

'What about trying more therapists?'

'I have gone to like, four or five of them. None of them have worked. I am telling you, I don't think India has good therapists. I have read so many bios and websites and what not, and they all seem crazy to me.'

'But you've been going only once a month…'

'She makes me wait two hours each time, and then asks me to talk to my pain. I really haven't been able to talk to that.'

'Do you want me to ask that friend for recommendations? Maybe there are better ones out there?'

'I guess,' I said.

Maybe the young people who'd done their master's abroad are plugged into a different world.

'Don't tell her you are asking for me. Say you are asking for a friend,' I added, my shame coming back as usual.

K sent me a list of contacts. I went through each one in minute detail. Googling them, checking their Facebook walls. I didn't want to waste any more time or money, nor did I have the emotional strength to recount everything that was wrong with my mind, or to go over my past all over again. As I cross-checked their qualifications, the rankings of their universities, and whatever else I could find on the internet, a memory came back to me, something a washing machine salesman had told me a few months earlier.

I had gone to an electronics store to buy an IFB washing machine on a friend's recommendation. At the store, the salesperson tried to dissuade me and showed me a brand-new Siemens model for the same price. I thought it was the usual salesman trick and insisted on IFB, but he said, 'It's made in India.'

I looked at him. 'But isn't Siemens also made in India?'

'IFB has tied up with Indian manufacturers, but Siemens is made in Germany and sent here. It's better.'

'I thought India had figured out manufacturing. "Make in India" and all that,' I said.

'Sir, India is India, and Germany is Germany.'

He grinned. I grinned. And I bought the Siemens machine he recommended.

I chose my therapist the same way I chose the washing machine: Dr R, with a Ph.D. in Psychology from the United States. She had a website with a list of publications, work experience, and clear guidelines. There were even some YouTube videos with titles like 'What to Do If Your Wife Earns More Than You.'

For a moment, I reconsidered. But then I thought, these were the problems of the Indians around me. Who was I to judge? She had an email ID listed, so I wrote to her. She called me back, asked about everything I was going through, and then sent me a form with terms of consent, emergency contacts, and past history. Here was someone who clearly had their act together. And if she had her act together, maybe she could help me get mine together too.

The added bonus was that her office was just fifteen minutes from mine.

I could see it in my mind's eye already: soon, I would be cured. I'd reach a time when I didn't think about cancer at all. I'd be able to sleep at night. Or take the stairs. Maybe even smoke a cigarette with my colleague during afternoon chai.

The only caveat was the cost. Her sessions were three times the price of my previous therapist, and she charged fifty percent of the fee for last-minute cancellations. But in that inflation, there was hope. This was, perhaps, the Apple version of therapy, overpriced, yes, but it got the job done. I would get what I was paying for.

The first meeting was spent creating a plan of action. Her office was on the ground floor of an apartment complex in suburban Mumbai. As I walked in, the watchman nodded at me, and maybe it was a sign of progress that I didn't care if he now knew I was a 'crazy' person who needed a therapist to feel better. The room was cozy, with a couch opposite a chair. It didn't have the Hollywood therapy-room vibe, but hurray, it was as close to beautiful as I could hope for.

When I went to the loo, I noticed there was no lock inside. I figured this was probably because some patients were so unwell they might get up to all kinds of shenanigans under the pretext of a pee. Still, she offered me green tea while we chatted and criticized my previous therapist for only meeting me once a month. Four times a month, she said, was needed for my level of anxiety.

For a moment, the middle-class part of my brain perked up: was this only a ploy to get more money? Possibly. But maybe I did need that level of intervention. At that point, I would have done anything to end those six months of hell.

If nothing else, my previous therapists had helped me order my thoughts. By now, I knew exactly how to tell my story, hitting the right emotional beats, offering the correct moments of revelation, and at the same time, showing just how difficult life had become.

'Aakash, do you know the cause of your anxiety?' she asked.

Oh no. Was this just going to be my previous therapist with better furniture?

'Because I think I'm dying of cancer?'

'That's true, but do you know the real reason?'

'I don't think so.'

She pulled a small whiteboard from behind her chair and drew a circle of arrows. One arrow was 'thoughts', another 'feelings', and the third had a question mark.

'Now do you know what that third arrow stands for?'

'No.'

'See, first you have a thought. That thought creates certain feelings. Those feelings create more thoughts, and that's what traps you in a cycle of anxiety.'

The arrows looped into each other like an ouroboros eating its own tail. I couldn't believe it, a therapist who actually answered her own questions in the first session. It was like finally getting to binge-watch a show after years of waiting for the weekly cliffhangers.

'What do you think we should do about this situation?' she asked.

'Perhaps…fight that original thought with some positive reinforcement?' I replied, like a schoolchild eager to please.

'Yes…that's one good technique, but in your case, it still leads to more feelings, which means more anxiety. So you have to reach a stage where you don't have the thought at all. When it comes into your mind, you must push it out at once.'

Unlike the previous advice, exercise, eat healthy, live with relatives, meditate, or 'talk to my pain', her homework felt doable. I was to maintain a journal of all my thoughts and feelings, which we would go through together. She also suggested I take a second opinion on my medication and even referred me to a doctor at a nearby hospital.

That day, as I walked out, I felt the warm glow one feels when encountering a true professional. It is no less sublime than watching a great work of art. Like finding a plumber who immediately knows what's wrong and fixes it without fuss, or an accountant who lays out a perfect investment plan and answers all your questions without sounding like a snake-oil salesman. Those moments are rare, but when they occur, they make the frightening world outside just a little more manageable.

17

Psychiatrist IV: A second opinion

The psychiatrist for my second opinion operated out of Hinduja Hospital, the same hospital where both my mother and grandmother had died. I couldn't decide if that was a comforting thought. My history with Bombay was long, but most of it was littered with memories like these. The happy moments were few and far between. I had once believed I could replace all this tragedy with some happiness, but that seemed far beyond my reach.

On the way to the hospital, I stopped for a chai and passed the doctor who had once told me that my mother could not be saved. He looked at me for a moment, his eyes softening. I wondered whether I should make small talk, but he hurried past, and I continued on, relieved.

At this enormous hospital, the process felt impersonal. I had to fill out a form, enter my name, create an account, pay before I could get an appointment, and then wait for an hour while the doctor finished his rounds. I felt a brief moment of fear that someone might recognize me. This was, after all, a Maharashtrian stronghold, and random relatives often turned up in such places. Once, a stranger had simply walked up to me, confirmed my surname, and asked, 'Are you running an Airbnb inside your home?' Another time, a woman had blurted out, without even a hello, 'You Karkare?' Moments like these had made me wary. People already pitied me, and if they now knew I was seeking psychiatric help, it would only deepen that pity. Thankfully, no such encounter took place that day. Still, I told myself I had to learn how not to think like this at all.

When I was finally called in, I saw a row of young interns standing behind the psychiatrist. He carried himself with the brisk air of a corporate professional. His credentials had been affirmed by a *Times of India* interview where he'd explained how he coped with the gloom of his job by lifting weights in the gym until he couldn't think anymore.

He asked me if I minded the interns observing. I looked at their eager, bright faces and said I didn't. If I could contribute in some small way to the greater project of understanding the human mind, I would do it. Perhaps sharing my story would also help lift the pointless burden of shame.

The psychiatrist himself was much like the others I'd met. He didn't take my struggles too seriously. Maybe he belonged to that generation that thought people like me were simply too weak. At times, I was inclined to agree with them, though such thoughts got me nowhere. He radiated the energy of a man for whom everything outside the most pressing matters was a burden on his time. Still, he offered me one piece of advice that stayed with me.

'See, my friend,' he began, 'the first question is, why does your mind fixate on cancer? There are so many illnesses one can die from. I could even make you a list of worse diseases…'

He paused when he saw my eyes widen in surprise, frightened by the suggestion that there might be diseases worse than cancer.

'Why I'm telling you this,' he continued, 'is to show that the fear is inside your head. That is why you're fixating only on cancer.'

I nodded. His twisted, macabre reasoning made sense to me. Yes, of course. Why cancer? Why not dementia, or some slower death?

'Will that be all?' he asked.

'No, actually. What about these prescriptions? Are they correct? My therapist sent me to double-check them with you.'

He glanced perfunctorily at the crumpled paper I handed

him, then looked straight into my eyes with a trace of derision.

'Look, my friend, these medications are fine. I could write you a different variety, but they'd do the same thing. However, if you cannot convince yourself, even they won't help you.'

I stared at him after this pronouncement. He nodded and grinned. Out of habit, I glanced at the students behind him. They looked at me as if I were some strange specimen, not yet having learned the poker face most mental health professionals wore. My revelation about my dead parents had already unsettled a few of them. The rest now absorbed details about my cancer dreams, insomnia, and six months of suffering. I could see the relief on their faces: at least it wasn't them.

'Well, thank you then,' I said.

'Great, take care. I'll speak to your doctor once,' he replied.

'Great, thanks.' I got up, feeling underwhelmed yet somewhat comforted by the sense of collaboration amongst professionals working on my cure.

I wondered why he carried so much derision for his own profession, even though he seemed to enjoy it. Perhaps he believed that minor issues, feelings, anxiety, were mostly nonsense, and that only those with truly serious problems needed real care. Maybe he was right but what good would that do for me?

18

Artemis

In my diary, I realized, to my dismay, that the feeling I kept coming back to was loneliness. To me, it felt like a kind of weakness. Since my parents had died and I wasn't close to any of my relatives, I had thought I would eventually find a community that could recreate that sense of family for me. That is why I held so much love for the stories of *Cahiers du Cinéma* of the French New Wave or Richard Linklater with his Austin Film Society that formed clubs of cinephile that created a sense of community. I believed that through media, I would meet kindred spirits, people I could share my true self with, people who, for once, might really understand me.

But my constant worries about what people thought of me, and my tendency to abandon myself in even the smallest interactions, prevented any kind of lasting connection. On top of this was my own conviction that I had seen and understood more than those who still had parents. Even the grown-ups at work, people I had wanted to see as surrogate parents or mentors, to fill the maternal and paternal void in my life, still complained about living with their parents.

Becoming an orphan in your twenties gives you a different perspective of the world. It made me rephrase the famous quote by C.L.R. James: *'What do they know of life who only a loving family know?'*

I thought that with mentors and friends, I would be able to stop living inside my head so much. With surrogate parents, I would have someone rooting for me in the world. With friends, I would have people to confide in about what bothered me, or simply someone to share a beer with while watching the IPL.

Even in my career, despite knowing my parents would never have understood the work I was doing, I felt a strange sense of loss. It was peculiar, because even people my age with living parents, especially in creative fields, were often 'orphaned' in a way. Their middle-class families didn't understand their choices or see their work as real careers. My case wasn't entirely different. Yet, there is something that separates my situation from theirs. Those who rebel against their parents can still blame them for their mistakes, can still wrestle with that force. It gives them momentum, even material for late-night bar conversations about how their Mom and Dad had fucked them up like Philip Larkin once wrote. But I had no one to blame but myself. The battle against existential despair was mine alone to bear.

S and my girlfriend tried to convince me otherwise, telling me it was normal, that many people lose parents. And through experience, I came to see that they were right. Quite a few people I met around my age had lost one parent, unlike the Sooraj Barjatya films where entire generations live together forever, interrupted only by the occasional fall from a staircase. Over time, my desire for connection lessened to a degree I had never experienced before. My therapy sessions followed a structured format: first, my journal would be read and discussed. It felt like a strange confrontation with my own shame, having someone else read my thoughts without judgement. Often, the entries revolved around my fears of cancer or death, and then we would move into strategies for fighting these worries, some through action, others through mental conditioning. It felt like one of those classic fantasy novels where a student sits with a sensei in a forest, learning the skills of the old masters on how to live.

She encouraged me to join classes, talk with colleagues, be more honest. I did those things, and they helped, but friendship is a process that takes years. How does one suddenly make friends in their twenties? At least I couldn't.

Once, a group of us at work shared a taxi to the station. On the way, we were talking about home. In response to a question I no longer remember, I said, 'I live alone.'

'So, you are not from Mumbai?' one of my colleagues asked.

'No, I am from here. Born and raised.'

I tried to keep my answers brief, hoping to shift the subject. But they didn't take the hint.

'Where are your parents?' another asked, their expression slowly darkening.

'They're dead,' I replied.

Silence followed. They looked at one another, wide-eyed with shock. I tried not to care. The taxi rolled on in heavy quiet until one of them, perhaps unable to bear it any longer, asked the most basic of questions: 'So…what do you do for food?'

'I cook for myself,' I said. Thankfully, the station arrived soon after and we parted ways.

At a writing workshop in Pondicherry, I thought I was finally amongst artists, people who might have seen the darker sides of life. But once again, my story turned the session into therapy for them. My reality seemed unimaginable, a reminder for them to spend time with their own parents while they still could. Someone even commented that my reluctance to talk about my parents suddenly 'made sense'.

At times, I wished I could carry around a sign: *Height: 6'6". Status: Orphan. Please don't ask, it hurts.* Sometimes, I even wanted to lie, say my parents had retired to the mountains, or moved abroad, anything to escape the awkwardness. But I stopped short of that. I decided I would wait until I was older, when it would seem more 'normal' to have dead parents. Still, I remember a man close to sixty, with parents in their nineties, saying to me: 'I can't imagine not having parents.'

Sometimes, though, I did lie. I told people my parents were running a textile business in the United States.

'No, Aakash, you must never lie,' Dr R said when I confessed.

'That means you haven't moved on. That means you aren't accepting your story.'

'But I can't handle how awkward people get.'

'That's their problem. You need to be honest. It's not as big a deal as you think.'

She often set me tasks—open up at work, reconnect with old friends. But I never managed much. Over the months, though, the loneliness that had haunted my twenties began to fade.

'So, did you make a friend this week?' Dr R asked one day.

'Not really,' I admitted. 'But I've stopped feeling the need.'

'How come?' she asked, surprised, because for so long, my journal entries had been consumed by that very longing.

To my embarrassment, an answer came to me. I wondered if I should lie, but then it would defeat the purpose.

'Ever since I have been coming here, I have somehow lost that urge.'

She looked a little disapproving, or awkward, or maybe it was my projection. What I had really wanted, and gotten nowhere else, was a space where I could finally unload everything I carried. Perhaps because I was paying someone, and by law I had privacy, it felt like the only place where it was safe to do so. I thought of my death anxiety, layered with health anxiety, layered with insomnia, as a kind of regular household problem, like a clogged sink. Finally, I had found someone with a good plunger.

After months of digging through all the crap in my brain, my therapist suggested we close this excavation of the past with letters to my parents, followed by another session where I would speak directly to them. Since I didn't keep photographs of the house, this meant placing an iPad and a phone on two chairs in front of me. It was a strange, almost mystical experience. But it didn't really work, I didn't believe in it. I even asked my therapist to leave, just to see if I could be comfortable doing something that felt both cringe-inducing and like the climactic, cathartic moment in a movie.

On the sofa, I placed the devices, googled 'Hemant Karkare' and 'Kavita Karkare' images, and asked the therapist to leave the room. I had revealed nearly everything by then, but there are always some things you can reveal to no one. I tried to force myself to cry, to let the pain come flooding out in a way that would free me forever. But nothing seemed to happen.

There are many stages of thinking about your parents after they die. Through most of my twenties, I was angry with them, angry that they were never there, angry that they had suddenly died before there could be any resolution. That anger left no space for grief. If I was so furious at them, why should I mourn them? I often thought to myself.

What would often bring tears, however, was the thought that two people who'd built a life of fifty years had suddenly vanished into the cosmos. Papa died for the failures of others, his work questioned without him there to defend it. And Mummy, just as she was beginning to live her life again. I had imagined her reaching her eighties, like her mother before her, becoming a jolly old woman, a repository of ancient wisdom and Marathi recipes.

Art insists there is neat resolution to grief. But there isn't. The pain remains just as raw. You only learn to live around it.

Reading became a way to connect with my parents, to step into their adult world that had always seemed distant, incomprehensible, and so unlike mine. When I read, I felt I was communing with my father and the generations before him. A few years after his death, I decided to read his favourite book: *Of Human Bondage*.

My mother once told me she had read *Of Human Bondage* when she was pregnant with me. When I read it at seventeen, Somerset Maugham's novel spoke to me deeply. As I turned its pages, a running commentary of questions filled my mind, an attempt to understand my father through this book, in ways he had never revealed himself to me in person.

I wondered how each of them had reacted to the novel. My father and I both identified with Philip. His twenties mirrored Philip's, wandering, trying new things, experimenting with life before settling down. Even after marriage, he continued to travel, exploring the world through his work.

But what about my mother? Who did she identify with? If it was Philip, did she rue the life she gave up? Or had she, like Philip at the end, made peace with it? Perhaps she didn't identify with him at all. Maybe it was one of the women in the novel. Most likely, it was Sally, the woman Philip marries in the end. But in these over-intellectualized speculations, there is always danger.

'Who did you like the most in *Of Human Bondage*,' I asked her soon after finishing the book.

'I read it many years ago. It was a good book, but now I don't remember much.'

My mother had a difficult relationship with her children reading. While she had encouraged it at first, leaving notes and chits all over the house so I learned reading and spelling earlier than most kids, later, she came to resent the decision to live in a house overflowing with books.

'I'm sorry I ever taught my kids to read,' she once yelled during a fight. 'Sorry I filled this house with books. Because of them, you became too intelligent, always analysing me and our relationship. If you had never read so much, you would have been good children, obedient children. You would have appeared for your Chartered Accountancy exams and wanted nothing more than to stay with me forever.'

Why was she so afraid of me becoming the person I had become?

S once told me, 'It all started when they put us in convent schools. Papa didn't want to. He said a Marathi school was just as good as any other. But Mummy couldn't speak English properly.

That's why she wasn't selected for TISS or SCM. So she wanted us to learn English, to master it. But she was always afraid it would drive us away. That a deep gap would grow between us, one she could never bridge. And it did.'

For most of my life, Marathi, my mother tongue, was the language of the annoying relative who gave unwanted advice and kept talking (read: lecturing) long after I stopped listening. It was the language of the never-ending religious ceremony, where one had to pretend to be solemn and serious, sitting in uncomfortable positions with no backrest as coils of smoke made an already sweltering room hotter. It was the language an incredibly strict tutor would come home to teach me for four hours a week in the evenings, hours stolen from my precious playtime. And yet, I suddenly found myself having fond memories of Marathi, of speaking it, of talking to people I liked in it, and I wanted to return to it. All the more so because every thread that tied me to my childhood and my past, my parents and all four grandparents, had been severed. In English, the language of the colonialists, I became a cold, hard logician, always seeking the rational solution to every problem. But in Marathi, I felt differently. I thought differently. I revealed a side of myself I didn't know existed.

The smallest things set off waves of nostalgia, opening floodgates of feelings I still don't fully know what to do with: watching Marathi recipe videos on YouTube starring kindly middle-aged women giving tips for my favourite childhood foods; stumbling across phrases I last heard as a child, now absent from my everyday life because I hardly speak Marathi anymore.

And I like this part of myself, the uncertain, vulnerable part, because English rarely provokes this kind of visceral reaction.

As I grow older and gain hindsight, I realize that parenting is perhaps far harder than I once believed. It's nothing like the easy version promised in family sitcoms or children's books. Everyone simply repeats a mixture of the parenting they received and whatever they're capable of giving. That realization, however, does not make forgiving or forgetting any easier.

I spent most of my twenties angry, at the government, at the BJP, at the right wing, at the media, at my own parents, at the people who kept asking me the same question over and over: 'Are you his son?' all to satisfy what seemed to me a vulgar curiosity.

I grieved the people I had lost. I grieved my own early adulthood, the days and nights stolen by anxiety. My emotions about all of this resembled Mumbai's buildings, constantly under renovation but never finished. All I could do was accept it.

Then came a turning point: the first day in my life when I didn't think about cancer. It was a year after the night of one hundred tiny ants on a weekday. A hot, muggy day. I went to work, ate *kheema pav* for lunch, took a cab home, and as I stepped out of the lift, drenched in sweat and exhaustion, I realized that I hadn't thought about impending doom for the entire day. I hadn't checked myself for symptoms. I hadn't thought about diabetes, hypertension, or any kind of cancer, not lung, blood, pancreatic, colon, or skin.

Therapy sessions continued through the year. Slowly, the trauma receded into the distance. But the pain lingered, so I quit my job. I no longer believed journalism or writing about movies was my calling. Anxiety had hollowed everything out. I wanted only one thing: freedom from it. If the job had truly satisfied me, perhaps the anxiety would never have bloomed in the first place. My love for movies faded away.

The gym became an unexpected ally, not in the way psychiatrists had prescribed, but in my own obsessive fashion. At first, I focused on losing weight. Then I began testing myself: lifting heavier weights, running faster on the treadmill, checking if I could do everything a healthy twenty-five-year-old should be able to do. Something that might reveal whether a hidden tumor lurked inside me. Eventually, I cleared myself through every test I could think of. I needed no further proof.

My therapist and I began running out of things to talk about. From weekly sessions, we dwindled to twice a month, and finally, once. I stopped taking my medications, partly out of fatigue with their side effects, partly out of laziness. Waiting hours in a clinic for a refill no longer felt worth it. To fill the silence, I spoke about my cat, Artie, and my irrational fear that she would die. To her credit, my therapist listened, though what could she really say to a grown man terrified that his cat might slip into the elevator shaft while he was at work?

I had adopted Artie during therapy. Both of us were orphans, I joked. The difference was that my parents had died, and hers had abandoned her in the rain for being the runt of the litter. I had wanted a pet, but feared responsibility. When I found her, frail and sickly, I told myself I'd nurse her back to health and release her back into the streets.

But our days fell into rhythm. I went to work and to therapy. Twice a day, I gave her medication, though the vet warned she might not survive. I panicked, convinced that losing her would only prove I was cursed. Instead, she survived, and thrived. She even killed a squirrel that had sneaked through the window. That's when I named her Artemis, Goddess of the Hunt. Artie, for short.

My anxiety shifted: Could she slip through the window grate and fall? Would she dart out of the door and down the elevator shaft? If she gained too much weight, would she develop kidney issues? Once, I accidentally fed her beer-battered squid rings, then panicked about the alcohol content. Google reassured me that the alcohol would have evaporated in cooking, but I still stayed awake, watching for signs of poisoning.

And yet, her presence was life itself. At night, if I heard noises, I checked Artie. If she stirred in her sleep beside me, I knew the house was safe. With Artie, I allowed myself emotions I had long suppressed since my parents' deaths. My upbringing had taught me to mistrust feelings, to see them as irrational, clouding judgement. But with her, emotion was allowed, this invisible bond between two orphans with no past. At last, I had one member in my 'orphan club'. Therapy shifted then: my flight anxiety, my hope to study abroad, my vague plans for a master's. Quitting my job no longer felt like failure, it felt like opening a door.

If life is a story, is it tragedy or comedy? Perhaps it depends on how you choose to see it. I liked to imagine mine as a comedy of errors. My relationship with my therapist began to resemble Woody Allen's line in *Annie Hall*: 'A relationship is like a shark. It has to constantly move forward or it dies. And I think what we got on our hands is a dead shark.'

I didn't know how to end things without offending her. I wasn't cured, but I was better, as good as I could be. I considered excuses: telling her I was moving abroad, or to another city. But life resolved it for me. I overslept, missed an appointment, ignored her texts for a day. She never followed up. Just like that, therapy ended. And I didn't relapse.

A few nights later, I stayed up watching *Aligarh*, recommended by a friend. The film, about a gay poet at Aligarh Muslim University persecuted by colleagues, left me shaken. Googling him later, I watched an interview where he spoke English with the same lilt my mother had, as though translating directly from Marathi. I found strange parallels with my parents—both had died fighting the system. Conspiracy theories trailed each of them. But I only wanted them to have lived freely, happily. The poet-professor was shortly to migrate to the United States. Pappa had wanted to begin writing books and enjoy his retirement. Mummy had begun enjoying travelling and hanging out with friends.

For the first time in a very long time, I wept. Tears for Mummy and Pappa, for their unfinished lives.

And in those tears, I found the catharsis I had been seeking for so long.

Epilogue
(2025)

'I'm surrounded by relics of a life that no longer exists.'

—Ruth Fischer, *Six Feet Under*

The shrill ring of the phone shattered the stillness of the evening. It was either the 19th or 20th of April, 2019. At my desk, I was deep in the throes of crafting my first novel while also translating books from Marathi to English. My thoughts often drifted to K, about to leave for a Ph.D. in the United Kingdom. The prospect of facing Mumbai's sprawling chaos alone, without her, loomed large. Yet, I was slowly coming to terms with it.

But now, this incessant ringing, a barrage of calls from countless unknown numbers, demanded my immediate attention.

Experience had taught me that whenever my phone erupted like this, it often involved my father. On fortunate days, the calls were harmless: a forgotten Amazon parcel or a spam call from ICICI Lombard. That evening, however, as I typed my father's name into Google, the results pointed to what I had dreaded. Pragya Singh Thakur, a BJP Lok Sabha candidate for Bhopal, had ignited her campaign by declaring that my father died because she had cursed him to death, a statement designed to court controversy and capture attention on the right-wing and national stages.

Thakur's outlandish claim, that she had cursed my father to death, was so absurd that it inadvertently lent credibility to conspiracy theories suggesting a collusion between saffron terror elements and the groups behind the Mumbai attacks.

The constant ringing of my phone was because I was the only family member residing in India. Confusion clouded my thoughts; I neither believed in curses nor entertained the petty disputes often sensationalized by the media. By sheer accident, I answered a call from a journalist, and we briefly discussed the situation. They insisted that the nation stood with me, urging me to make a public statement. Yet, what was there to really say? Denouncing the absurd claim that someone had cursed my father to death seemed pointless. Besides, it seemed like I had been on the Hemant Karkare beat longer than all the journalists who had been calling me. Pragya Singh Thakur had been making assertions of a similar nature for a while before 2019.

I wanted to express that the real journalistic duty lay in probing the intentions behind politicians' statements, in questioning why the BJP had nominated a terror-accused candidate. Instead, the focus was on soliciting a reaction from his family. Silence also prevailed amongst most in the police force, those whose words carried real weight. On the anniversary of 26/11, they would press me to attend media events, exploiting my father's memory for PR while rarely standing by him.

Finally, the IPS organization issued a statement, a small relief in the chaos. Meanwhile, Maharashtra Chief Minister Devendra Fadnavis distanced themselves from the remarks. However, no one within the BJP took steps to challenge her candidacy. As ever, politics remained a game of mere posturing.

That year marked a pivotal shift; what were once considered fringe elements within the BJP had evidently moved into the mainstream. Yogi Adityanath ascended to the role of Uttar Pradesh Chief Minister in 2017, and by 2019, Pragya Singh Thakur had taken her seat in Parliament. The news of her election solidified a profound disconnection I felt from my own country, a disconnection that had been brewing and became irrevocable.

In the weeks leading up to her victory, I grappled with a troubling thought: was my silence born out of fear? A Facebook post found its way on my timeline, claiming that the Karkare children were most likely silent because they feared they would be killed if they spoke out. Obviously, I didn't believe such conspiratorial talk, because if you believe such things then, can you really believe in anything?

It wasn't fear, though, but a deep-seated sense of hopelessness that silenced me. The forces my father had valiantly opposed seemed to be prevailing, and the secular vision of India he championed appeared to be fading. This battle felt intensely personal.

I found myself seeking an escape from a reality where elected officials could unironically discuss death curses as a serious political stance, two decades into the 21st century. It was a surreal and disheartening backdrop against which I contemplated my place and my voice within my homeland.

The election of Pragya Singh Thakur and the surrounding media furore had unearthed aspects of my parents' lives that had always left me uneasy. I had encountered mostly the drawbacks of their visibility, scrutiny, controversy, and the relentless invasion of privacy. These experiences shaped a perspective where the negatives seemed to far outweigh any potential positives. It was difficult to see any benefit in the public exposure, even as a form of speaking up, when it often meant dealing with backlash or misrepresentation, making me question if there could truly be a favourable aspect to living one's life in the public eye.

I felt completely alone in that summer and on a whim applied to a master's programme in Creative Writing at the University of East Anglia (UEA) in UK, where K was also going to study.

Barring a brief upswing in her political career, which saw her join a parliamentary committee on defence under Rajnath Singh, Pragya Singh Thankur's controversial statements continued. They ranged from promoting cow urine as a cure for cancer to labelling Nathuram Godse a patriot. Prime Minister Narendra Modi reportedly never forgave her for this remark, and she was denied a ticket for the 2024 elections. By 2025, the Bombay High Court had permitted a fringe organization to confer Pragya Singh Thakur with an award in Malegaon. In July of that year a Special NIA court acquitted her and six others of all charges in the Malegaon Blasts case.

∽

The first few months in the UK were pleasant. K and I loved our new home, rented from an American professor at UEA who also taught at Azim Premji University. We had a back garden and enjoyed walking to our local Indian shop, run by a kindly Malayali man, and cooking for one another. I loved the huge library at UEA, where I spent long hours reading and writing. Slowly, I became comfortable calling myself a writer, and even telling other people that I was one. No one stared at me as I walked through the streets of Norwich. No one in a government office looked twice at my surname. I was simply Aakash, free to be whoever I wanted to be.

When the first semester assignments were due, I procrastinated until the last minute and then, overnight, managed to blast out a 1,500-word piece about my health anxiety and my misadventures navigating the Indian mental health system. Over the rest of the year, I continued building on that memoir, finding the process strangely therapeutic. I kept telling myself I would never publish it. Alongside it, I worked on translations and wrote my novel in the library. In class, I shared only glimpses of my mental health experiences. Everything about my parents, I couldn't bring myself to write.

Over the years, even though K and I had been each other's best friends, knowing one another like few others could, and she was my only family alongside Artie, who was staying with K's parents, we had become less a couple and more a friendship. Those years had taken a toll on our relationship, one I had tried not to see until then. K could no longer see me apart from my anxiety. Once, when I was discussing the memoir with her, she asked, 'How long will you think about all this stuff?'

'I don't know,' I said. 'I guess, as a writer, I'd like to write about death and mortality.'

Her face fell.

By the end of the master's programme, COVID-19 struck, and we were trapped inside a tiny studio apartment in Norwich. We began doing the very things we had promised we'd never do, having long, thunderous arguments over small things like washing the dishes or mopping the floor.

When we first moved to Norwich, K and I had thought we might apply for a spousal visa so I could stay on after my master's. But neither of us felt comfortable with that option. I didn't want to rely on her to that extent, and I also wanted her to have the chance to enjoy life as a student in the UK on her own.

Back home, though, there was Pragya Singh Thakur, elected an MP despite having once said she had cursed my father to death. The thought of returning to India filled me with dread. I was convinced all my anxieties would come rushing back. Yet there was no other option. By the end of 2020, K and I agreed that our relationship was no longer working. On my last night in Norwich, we sat next to each other in bed, holding hands. I cried longer and harder than I had since I was a boy in school, forgotten at pick-up by my parents.

I spent a month alone in London before finally returning to Mumbai, unsure of what awaited me.

~

For a few months, life was good. I had several projects going on simultaneously. Oddly enough, COVID had been a good thing. Plenty of time to write, and I had no older family members to worry about. That is when the second wave happened in India, and the grief of the breakup with K struck me with full force, like a bullet that had been travelling in slow motion that had finally reached its target, scattering shrapnel in every direction. There was no way to distract myself. It was me, at home, alone with the walls of my house.

Thankfully, I no longer feared nightly intruders. Though I never figured out how that completely went away. I took to smoking in the streets, finding that the local cigarette seller had relocated to the courtyard of an abandoned building deemed unsafe. Smokers from around the neighbourhood gathered there, hiding from the authorities, sitting on the steps of a structure that could collapse at any moment. Strangely, I felt a sense of community amongst them. Smoking worked as a salve against anxiety. People would grin at me when I came by, and eventually one of the men spoke up, saying he remembered me from our cricket days. He told everyone I was Hemant Karkare's son and asked why I wasn't writing a book about it.

I returned to therapy and medication to face the grief again. This time, I was more familiar with the process. My old therapist recommended a new one, and I found a young psychiatrist nearby for prescriptions. With my new therapist, I finally gained a different perspective on the world. In that past relationship, I had been clinging to an older version of myself, one I no longer wanted. Letting go of that Aakash meant acknowledging the relationship wasn't working. Therapy gave me permission to rediscover what I had been seeking all along—the optimism of my early twenties. It was tied to all that magical thinking of living in the moment, focusing on the now, and so on. It may sound clichéd, but for me it was freeing in a way nothing else had been.

It was during this period that I felt compelled to begin my memoir. For years I had tried to write a novel, but this story demanded to be told, as if it wouldn't release me until I put it down on paper. Focusing on the personal in the wake of the 26/11 attacks might seem narcissistic to some, but to me, it felt essential. It was about what happens after the cameras turn off, after the headlines fade. It was about the lived reality, the unseen, unreported details that shape us. Over time, it began to feel like a political act: a refusal to let the public or opportunistic politicians claim our narratives.

At the core of media narratives lay a fundamental dehumanization of those involved. Once someone becomes a 'story', it's easy to forget they are real people living through it. In the age of social media, we see this constantly, videos go viral, snap judgements are made, and those depicted are rarely granted the benefit of the doubt. Journalists, too, by highlighting certain aspects of a person's life to craft a narrative, participate in this dehumanization. The drive to produce a compelling story, to ensure paragraphs flow and the prose shines, often distorts reality. When I shared excerpts of my memoir with an English writer and memoirist who taught a seminar during my master's, she remarked, 'You're trying to show people that this doesn't bother you anymore. You're putting it out of yourself.'

Friends often asked me, when I mentioned writing a memoir, 'Why you? At this age?'

My answer was simple: I believed I had a story to tell. A narrative I wanted to correct. Memories I wanted to preserve. I once emailed a noted Marathi author and translator, confessing my concern that I was too young to write about myself. True to her reputation for encouraging writers, she replied: 'Even those who are ninety haven't had these experiences.'

Those words were enough to convince me my story deserved to be told.

Somehow, the past no longer bore down on me with the same weight. I can't quite pinpoint what prompted this shift. Perhaps simply the act of growing older, crossing into my thirties, and finding a newfound confidence and self-assurance. This part of my life, once so defining, no longer demanded the significance I had once granted it. Physical distance from Mumbai, from Dadar TT, something my sisters sometimes found traumatic, also reshaped my perspective.

I had kept much of my parents' old furniture over the years: the sofa where my mother once sat, the bookcases and study tables, a dining table meant for five in a house where I now lived alone, and the ornate wooden double bed from my parents' room, complete with matching bedside tables. These items weren't preserved out of sentimentality; I had simply never gotten around to replacing them. The boot of my mother's old Swift Dzire still carried my father's police uniform, which the department hadn't wanted back. I kept putting off the decision of what to do with it. I wasn't ready to turn it into a shrine, yet I couldn't bring myself to throw it away. When I moved to Hindu Colony, I asked the police if they wanted these objects, but they refused. So I left them in the boot of the Swift Dzire, unwilling to bring them into the house, where they felt like an ominous presence. Later, I discovered that the Mumbai Police had refused to reuse the Toyota Qualis in which Pappa had spent his final moments, for the same reason.

Both my parents had died young and suddenly, leaving no plans, no final letters, not even a will. They left behind countless possessions no one knew what to do with. My mother, a hoarder, had kept everything connected to the past—old phones, broken laptops, unread books, ill-fitting clothes, documents that could easily aid identity theft, and faded bedsheets.

Then, after turning thirty-two in 2023, something shifted again. I was in a happy relationship with Z. I found myself finally comfortable enough to face a task I had long avoided. I had never wanted to live in Hindu Colony forever, and so I had never renovated the house since first moving in.

I bought a new bed and a cupboard to replace the rusty Godrej I had relied on for years. Until then, I thought I would eventually leave Dadar, leave Mumbai altogether, so I hesitated to make any permanent changes. But this time it felt necessary to renew the tangible pieces of my past. That decision sparked a transformative process: I removed every piece of furniture that carried the imprint of my parents' existence.

That first night, lying in a new bed in a room free of echoes from my past, I felt an overwhelming release. Around this furniture, no long arguments had been made, no one had died, no one had grieved, and no one had recounted their sorrow. The shadows that lingered seemed to lift, clearing a space both physically and mentally. In that newfound clarity, this version of my book, long suppressed, trapped within memory and inherited objects, finally began to pour out.